■ **Advance praise for *Dangerous Airwa***

"Scripture teaches that in the providence of ⌣⌣⌣, ⌣⌣⌣⌣⌣⌣⌣ arise in order to establish the right by negation, in order that those who are approved may be made manifest. Although Harold Camping's doctrine has troubled the church in the past, and has grown increasingly troubling, I am very grateful for James White's new book *Dangerous Airwaves*. This book shows that the truth is more than true—it is also clear."

—Douglas Wilson, Pastor
Author of *The Federal Husband* and *Future Men*

"Harold Camping's attack on the Church has harmed individuals, hurt congregations, and hampered media ministries that honor Christ and his Bride. James White demolishes Camping's distortions, and calls us to value the Church as much as Christ does."

—David Feddes, "The Back to God Hour"
(formerly aired on Family Radio)

"Mr.Camping's 'dead Church' doctrine is only really dangerous to those who don't know the truth, who have not been rooted and grounded in Christ, nor taught to rightly divide the word of truth. Nevertheless, faithful men on the front lines of God's Glory must expose him and all other false teachers. The honor of Christ and the safety of his lambs are at stake. Dr.White is very capable of doing just that!"

—Pastor Jesse Gistand, Grace Bible Church, San Leandro, CA
(former co-elder with Harold Camping
at the Reformed Bible Church, Alameda, CA)

"James White's work, *Dangerous Airwaves,* shows the whole diabolical scheme of Harold Camping from his invalid hermeneutics to his misuse of the original languages of the Bible and more. Speaking as one ex-Campingite, this book reveals the folly of Camping and must be read by those who want to know 'What saith the Scriptures' not 'What saith Camping.'"

—Dave Rastetter, Deacon, Faith Presbyterian Church,
Akron, Ohio (owner of http://www.familyradioiswrong.com)

"I am grateful to James White for setting the record straight on Harold Camping's views. We desperately need this kind of theological precision in a day when errors and heresies are underestimated."

—Joel Beeke, President
Puritan Reformed Theological Seminary

"Heresy is always a stealing of some Christian rags to cover heathen nakedness! Harold Camping is sewing a new fig leaf to cover his abhorrent privates by trying to establish a new Romanism with Family Radio as the cathedral, and he the self-appointed new Pope. But careful, biblical examination reveals 'this Emperor has no clothes.' After his failed prophecy that Christ was returning in 1994—he has resorted to another Edenistic pursuit: the demise, dismantling, and extinction of the local church. This is pure folly— Christianity by Howard Stern—and is comical except for the thousands who have unwittingly adopted it as orthodox.

"Dr. James White, once again, has proven to be a valuable, biblical, prophetic voice to the church today. He wields, as a skilled surgeon, the razor sharp scalpel of sound theological and doctrinal truth by exposing the gangrenous, factious, heretical teachings of Camping. As only a faithful shepherd in the church can do, he has instructed in sound doctrine and refuted those who contradict. This is a must read, especially for pastors, elders, and deacons. I highly commend it to you."

—Steve Camp, Christian Recording Artist (2 Cor. 4:5–6)

"James White effectively corrects teaching that has taken families out of churches like mine. The author expounds church truth and proper biblical interpretation. He exposes Mr. Camping's teaching as false, both in general and in specifics. Dr. White extensively refutes both Mr. Camping's written and spoken material. Mr. Camping wrongly advises people to leave God-honoring churches. Dr. White rightly advises people to leave dishonoring teaching against God's Word and His church."

—Dr. John Michael Thomas, Pastor
The Bible Church of Port Washington, Long Island, NY

"As pastor of a church that has twice experienced the departure of groups of families who have been seduced by the teachings of Harold Camping, I am thankful for James White's work in faithfully exposing and refuting the bizarre notions of this modern cult leader. Dr. White also presents a refreshingly clear and forthright presentation of the vital place of the church in the plan of God (especially when we remember that the historic Protestant confession has been that 'outside the visible church there is no ordinary possibility of salvation.'). Read this book to understand the 'Camping Captivity' of Family Radio. Use this book to help protect Christ's sheep from a dangerous wolf that comes into so many homes 'not sparing the flock.'" (Acts 20:29)

—William Shishko, Pastor
Orthodox Presbyterian Church, Franklin Square, New York

"As a pastor who has recently watched church members leave the Good Shepherd for the false teaching of Mr. Camping, I am grateful for Dr. White's insightful and lucid analysis. The heresy described within is a new brand of terrorism that threatens the flock of Christ and damages her witness in this world. This book not only effectively exposes this error; it will also serve to encourage you to rejoice in the truth, the truth of the Scriptures that belong to the church, the eternal Bride of Christ."

—Pastor Mark Stewart, Pastor
Covenant Reformed Church of Newton, NJ

"Radio is a powerful medium for the distribution of the Gospel. Unfortunately, as Dr. White points out in *Dangerous Airwaves*, there are radio teachers such as Harold Camping who, once a shepherd, has become a wolf and is leading the sheep astray."

—Dan Craig, General Manager
WRFD Radio, Columbus, Ohio
(Family Radio Employee, 1977–1980)

■ DANGEROUS AIRWAVES!

■ Dangerous Airwaves!

*Harold Camping Refuted
and Christ's Church Defended*

JAMES R. WHITE

2002 ■ Calvary Press, Amityville, New York

CALVARY PRESS PUBLISHING
Post Office Box 805
Amityville, NY 11701
1-800-789-8175
www.calvarypress.com

Book design and typography by Studio E Books
Santa Barbara, CA www.studio-e-books.com

Cover illustration by Chris Arnzen

White, James R.
   Dangerous airwaves! : Harold Camping refuted and Christ's church defended / by
James R. White.
   ISBN 1-879737-49-3
Suggested subject headings:
      1. Christianity—doctrines.
      2. Religion
      I. Title

10 9 8 7 6 5 4 3 2 1

■ Contents

Foreword

Words fail me as I attempt to convey my deepest thanks and appreciation to Dr. James White for the supreme service that he has rendered to the Church of Jesus Christ through the publication of *Dangerous Airwaves*. Writing in a respectful and riveting style easily understood by both leaders and laity alike, Dr. White has well addressed the most significant errors in Mr. Harold Camping's teaching, which are causing such spiritual detriment and significant destruction within Christ's Church. As a pastor who has personally experienced the pain of witnessing a number of people removing themselves from church membership and subsequently refusing to worship with any local congregation solely based upon Mr. Camping's harmful hermeneutic, I believe that this book could not have come at a better time!

Although I, along with many others, are no longer participating in Family Radio Bible Conferences or broadcasts, my sincere hope and fervent prayer is that the reading of this articulate defense of the truth will be greatly and graciously used of God for His glory. It is hoped that through this book many will return to their spiritual senses and have a greater appreciation and understanding of the Church which Christ purchased at the price of His blood.

—Pastor Rich Kuiken
Pompton Plains Reformed Bible Church, NJ
(former *Family Radio* Conference speaker & radio evangelist)

■ DANGEROUS AIRWAVES!

Introduction

There simply wasn't anything on my normal Christian radio station worth listening to, so I hit the "scan" button as I drove down the road. Various stations zoomed by until a deep, slow-moving, sonorous voice said something about God. I stopped the scan and began to listen. The man was talking to a caller, so I turned up the volume. I waited for the next caller and listened carefully. The question was a good one, and I immediately began thinking about how I would respond if I received such a call. I could not help but notice the host spoke slowly, and seemed not to hear the caller very well, either. At first the answer went along the same lines I would have given. But then, all of a sudden, it took a hard right turn: the host brought up an Old Testament passage that in its context was completely irrelevant to the question. It contained a reference to a number, and the host began expounding upon the numerological significance of that number as it related to his understanding of the question. I chuckled a bit, shook my head, and moved on.

I had heard vague comments over the years about one Harold Camping, but this was the first time I actually heard him speak. I did not know of anyone in my own fellowship that listened to him, I took only a passing interest in the uproar that developed over his 1994 prediction. As he had little impact in my local area, and as I had not, at that time, begun to travel extensively in ministry, I simply listed him as yet another false teacher who fell into the trap of date setting.

Then I began visiting Long Island to engage in the "Great Debate" series. It did not take long to start hearing about the impact Harold Camping's prediction of 1994 had had on the local churches in the New York area. As I spoke to pastors over lunch or dinner I began to realize that Camping had caused a tremendous problem in that area with his teachings. This was when I began to understand that Harold Camping held a sway over people that was far beyond what I had imagined from my brief exposures to him on Family Radio in Phoenix.

But, it was now post-1994, and surely everyone could see that he had been discredited. And yet, as I traveled about, I kept running into people who would ask me, "What do you think about Harold Camping?" I found the question troubling, as surely anyone would now realize that he was a false teacher. He had not repented of his 1994 prediction, and yet there were still people who were intent upon listening to him. There was obviously something more at work here than the simple popularity of a radio teacher or preacher. He had "followers" who, as I was starting to see, took on particular characteristics, not only in their theology, but also in their behavior and mannerisms!

While observing Harold Camping's followers might be somewhat interesting, in light of all the work in apologetics, writing, and teaching I was involved in, I truly did not have the time, nor the inclination, to pursue the matter. That is, until I was informed of his "new teaching" in the summer of 2001.

I received an email from a close friend who lives on Long Island, informing me that Camping was now teaching that the "church age has ended" and, though he was not, in the comments that were at that time airing, nearly as firm in his teachings as he is today, it was plain that this new teaching amounted to a full frontal assault upon the church of Jesus Christ.

I took the time to obtain tapes of Camping's explanations, and began to see that this new movement touched upon all my "issues of passion," that is, points of truth that I am passionate about defending and proclaiming. Camping's teaching attacks the church, and I am a churchman. It also attacks the clarity and authority of the Word of God (Camping's allegorical interpretation robs the Word of its original meanings and replaces them with his "spiritual" interpretations), and I love the Word of God. And he was presenting his teaching publicly, inviting a public, apologetic response.

And so I undertook to provide an apologetic, yet pastoral, response to Camping's attack upon Christ's Body, the Church. The task is not an easy or an enjoyable one on many levels. I do not personally enjoy listening to hours of Harold Camping's teachings on the Internet or by tape. But my true desire in this work is to encourage and edify the church, and if helping believers to see that Camping has completely missed the truth of the Word on the issue of the church will lead to the strengthening of that body, I am privileged to be given the opportunity.

It should be noted that no matter how diligently I may seek to represent the current state of Harold Camping's teachings, it is impossible to produce a published work that can keep up with the ever changing and developing "insights" of someone who honestly seems to believe that he is "seeing" things in Scripture that no one has ever seen before. Indeed, as I listen to the first response I made to Mr. Camping only last year, I can see how he has changed his emphases and some of his arguments in the intervening months. Surely the future will bring more changes (indeed, we can hope the future would bring an utter repudiation of his teaching and repentance on his part). Sadly, there are some who will reject any response to Camping on the basis that "you didn't deal with argument X" where "X" represents any one of thousands of comments and "insights" found in hundreds of Open Forum broadcasts, or Family Radio publications. But for those who understand the foundational aspects of Camping's teachings, this response should be to the point and useful.

This work is organized so as to provide as full orbed a reply as possible in a very limited space. That is, the fundamental issue (positively, the teaching of the perpetuity of Christ's visible church on earth, and negatively, the error of Camping's allegorical interpretation) will be addressed first. Then, in the second section, answers will be offered to the most commonly repeated arguments Camping (and his followers) are presenting *at this time*. If a passage is not addressed, it is probably because Mr. Camping did not "see" it as relevant during the writing of this work.

The impact of Camping's teaching against the church can be far-reaching. I have witnessed the heartbreak of pastors who have seen families sadly leave the fellowship, closing their ears to reason, following the siren call of Camping's allegorical interpretations into the dark confusion of the "fellowships." And though the church will always come through such attacks stronger than before, the pain in the lives of those deceived by Camping will be great. Restoration will come in the future for many (Camping's teaching simply cannot last), but it will be a long process, demanding much pastoral oversight and repentance. In the meantime, local churches will suffer the loss of people to a teaching that has no basis in Scripture whatsoever.

Surely Camping's call to flee from the church has caused many to re-evaluate their view of the church. Many of us have already had to repent of worldly ideas about the church, and have been called to again realize the importance of the church as it is revealed in the New Testament. If Camping's errors result in the saints once again treasuring the privilege of service in the body of Christ, then as always, God will be glorified even in this. May it be so!

Before the Battle Begins:
God's Word on the Church

The church of Jesus Christ is a divinely instituted organization that is central to the purposes of God. Every follower of Christ is called to serve within her fellowship, give his or her life for those who stand alongside in her membership, revel in the blessings of God poured upon her from on high, and seek to pass from this world into God's presence having promoted her work and standing on earth. A man's attitude toward the church says much of his spiritual health and maturity. The one who longs to be amongst God's people in worship, in singing, in proclamation, in the celebration of baptism and the Supper, has in that longing a sign of grace and the work of the Holy Spirit, for outside of religious hypocrites who do not last long where the Word is faithfully preached, the unregenerate man has no desire for these things, and finds them to be utter foolishness.

Do these words sound strange to you? They should not. The Scriptures are filled with teaching on the nature, purposes, mission, and perpetuity, of the Body of Christ, the Bride of Christ, and the church of the living God. One must be purposefully seeking to avoid exposure to the truths of the Bible to miss the repetitive references to Christ's Bride, the church. The teaching about her is often bound up with the very proclamation of the gospel, for it has always been God's will that every person He calls into fellowship with His Son is to take his or her place in the fellowship of that body for which He died, that visible entity that proclaims His name and worships in sprit and in truth.

The task at hand demands that we focus upon one particular aspect of the Bible's teaching on the church, that being its perpetuity.

However, to properly understand this truth we must lay a wider foundation in the more general teaching concerning the assembled body of believers, the church.

■ The Pillar and Foundation

One of the saddest statements I have ever read came from the pen of a person who converted to Roman Catholicism from the Orthodox Presbyterian Church. This person spoke of their "shock" at reading 1 Timothy 3:15 for the first time and considering the nature of the church. How a person could be very involved in the OPC and not know of this tremendous description of the church recorded in the Bible is truly a mystery; even more of a mystery is why this would "shock" any true disciple in the first place. But every believer should not only confess, believe in, and defend the divine truth enunciated in this passage, but the words should serve as a bulwark, a foundation upon which we stand. Hear the Word of the Lord:

> but in case I am delayed, *I write* so that you will know how one ought to conduct himself in the household of God, which is the church of the living God, the pillar and support of the truth. (NASB)

The Apostle Paul writes to Timothy and gives him instruction, as an elder in the church (probably at Ephesus), on the manner of conduct that should prevail in the fellowship of the church. Note that conduct is something that speaks to behavior within the visible church, the organized body with elders and deacons. The preceding context is all about elders and deacons and the everyday activity of the church as an organized body of believers. *The description of the church as the church of the living God is first and foremost a description of the church as she exists in the local body of believers.* This is a vital point.

Sound exegesis requires us to look closely at Paul's words and the context in which his child in the faith, Timothy, would have understood them. One vital point to keep in mind when reading Paul's letters to Timothy is seen in the common source both used in their teaching and preaching: the Greek Septuagint (the LXX), the Greek translation of the Tanakh, the Old Testament. Both used the same source in their teaching and preaching, and therefore, when we find Paul using terms that come directly from the LXX, we should be quick to realize that Timothy, being a student of the Scriptures himself (2 Timothy 3:14–15), would likewise make the same connections. And what do we find when we look at the terms Paul uses in this passage?

The first thing we discover is that the terms Paul uses are echoed in the pages of the Old Testament Scriptures. He speaks of the church as the "household of God." David had used the very same language long before. In 1 Chronicles 29:3 we read:

> Moreover, in my delight in the house of my God, the treasure I have of gold and silver, I give to the house of my God, over and above all that I have already provided for the holy temple.

These words were spoken, of course, in the context of the temple of God that was to be built in Jerusalem. This temple became the focus of the worship of the one true God. In the same way the church is the place where the central focus is the worship of God through the reading of the Scriptures, prayer, and the singing of God's praises. God is glorified and praised in His church, throughout the ages, as we will see in Paul's exposition to the church at Ephesus.

In a similar way the phrase "the living God" would have evoked a number of images in Timothy's mind, including these:

> But the LORD is the true God; He is the living God and the everlasting King. At His wrath the earth quakes, And the nations cannot endure His indignation. (Jeremiah 10:10)

> 'For who is there of all flesh who has heard the voice of the living God speaking from the midst of the fire, as we *have*, and lived? (Deuteronomy 5:26)

> My soul thirsts for God, for the living God; When shall I come and appear before God? (Psalm 42:2)

> My soul longed and even yearned for the courts of the LORD; My heart and my flesh sing for joy to the living God. (Psalm 84:2)

Joshua said, "By this you shall know that the living God is among you, and that He will assuredly dispossess from before you the Canaanite, the Hittite, the Hivite, the Perizzite, the Girgashite, the Amorite, and the Jebusite. (Joshua 3:10)

Then David spoke to the men who were standing by him, saying, "What will be done for the man who kills this Philistine and takes away the reproach from Israel? For who is this uncircumcised Philistine, that he should taunt the armies of the living God?" (1 Samuel 17:26)

In each of these passages the phrase "the living God" contrasts the true God of Israel with the false idols of the surrounding nations. It contains an implicit assertion of monotheism and a denial of the existence of *any* true God outside of Yahweh (cf. Isaiah 43:10). The living God is greatly concerned about His worship and His glory (all idols are, by nature, unconcerned about such things, and those who control the worship of such abominations are the ones who are manipulating people to their own ends), and by drawing from this Old Testament terminology, Paul is continuing to emphasize the continuity between God's revelation of old and this new work, that of the church.

He continues the motif by describing the church as the "pillar and foundation of the truth." The word he chooses for "pillar" is used a number of times in the LXX. In Exodus 13:22, 14:19, and 33:9 the pillar of cloud/fire, representing God's presence and protection, uses this term. And in 1 Kings 7:15 the bronze pillars in the Temple are described using the same word.

When we listen, then, with the full effect of the background of the Old Testament in place, to the description Paul gives of the church in 1 Timothy 3:15, we can hear it at the "volume" it would have carried in its original context. Remember, Paul is exhorting young Timothy in both his letters to him to stand strong in the service of Christ within the church. We are encouraged to give our best in the pursuit of the highest goals and the most exalted service, so Paul reminds Timothy of what he had surely already taught him in person. The church is the household of God, under His divine and sovereign rule. It is a divine institution, established at the command of God, sustained by His Spirit. And the church has a purpose as a result: it is the firm, unmoving ground upon which the truth can stand without fear of falling to the ground. The terms "pillar and foundation" speak to the strength of the church in providing a ground upon which the truth can be based. Surely for young Timothy this would be a great encouragement, but do not forget that for Paul this would be just as great a boon, for he was facing the end of his life, and could not but consider the future, filled with challenges and dangers, and pray for the continuing health of the young church. He had confessed to the Corinthians that there was upon him the "daily pressure of concern for all the churches" (2 Corinthians 11:28), so surely that had not ended when he wrote to Timothy. And yet he knew the truth: the church would endure because it is not a merely human institution; it is divine in its very nature. God had decreed the church to function as the ground and support of the truth, holding forth the word of life and worshipping Him who is truth itself. This did not make the church the truth itself (indeed, Paul's epistles, written to churches, almost always have corrective elements, demonstrating the constant need for reformation in the fellowship), but the intimate relationship between the true church and the truth itself is unmistakably taught in Scripture.

■ The Heart of God's Revelation of the Church

As Paul was imprisoned at Rome he wrote to his beloved churches. One of those letters, the epistle to the Ephesians, is most unique. It was evidently meant to be circulated around the Lycus River valley and the province of proconsular Asia, of which Ephesus was the capital. In this letter Paul opens up vital and important themes relating to the gospel and the church. One could hypothesize that the great apostle, facing what could be his final hours, chooses to address issues of great significance so that those who continue the work of the church in future generations would have true, abiding, *and unchanging* apostolic instruction.

Through the first three chapters of this work Paul knits together the highest revelation of God's purpose in the gospel *and* the relationship that gospel bears to the church. In the first chapter he speaks of God's eternal choice of the elect, and His provision, in Christ, for their salvation. This leads to the tremendous apostolic prayer of Ephesians 1:16ff, wherein he prays for the spiritual enlightenment of his audience so that they might know the depths of

God's power and glory. The climax of the prayer comes in the recognition of Christ as the head of the church, "which is His body, the fullness of Him who fills all in all" (1:23). But without any interruption in thought Paul moves directly from this back into specifics regarding the work of God in the salvation of His people (2:1–10).

Many evangelicals know the words of Ephesians 2:8–10 by heart. This great summary of the gospel, the centrality of grace, the freedom of God's power and His sovereign purpose, is followed immediately by verses not nearly so well known, for the Apostle immediately places the work of salvation in the context of the church: those who receive the great benefits of God's grace are, *by that very work of grace,* joined together in the body of Christ. Note his words:

> But now in Christ Jesus you who formerly were far off have been brought near by the blood of Christ. For He Himself is our peace, who made both *groups into* one and broke down the barrier of the dividing wall, by abolishing in His flesh the enmity, *which is* the Law of commandments *contained* in ordinances, so that in Himself He might make the two into one new man, *thus* establishing peace, and might reconcile them both in one body to God through the cross, by it having put to death the enmity (Ephesians 2:13–16).

One of the most striking elements of this passage, at least for the person who "pigeon-holes" the doctrines of salvation and the church so that they are utterly separate entities (seen in the "I can be saved but have nothing to do with the church" attitude of many evangelicals), is the intertwining of the themes of redemption and church. The barrier between Jew and Gentile is broken down in the common means of salvation God uses, the cross of Jesus Christ. The two groups are made one in the fellowship of the church by the work of Christ who abolished the enmity *in His flesh*. The blood, the flesh, the establishment of peace—-these are all terms of redemption yet they are used by Paul in the context of the *church*. Why emphasize this? It is impossible to separate the proclamation of the gospel of Jesus Christ from God's purpose to gather those redeemed within the church of Jesus Christ. We will see the importance of this fact in light of our main purpose, the examination of Harold Camping's teachings.

The unity brought about by the gospel between Jew and Gentile continues as Paul's theme,

> So then you are no longer strangers and aliens, but you are fellow citizens with the saints, and are of God's household, having been built on the foundation of the apostles and prophets, Christ Jesus Himself being the corner *stone,* in whom the whole building, being fitted together, is growing into a holy temple in the Lord, in whom you also are being built together into a dwelling of God in the Spirit (Ephesians 2:19–22).

The church of Jesus Christ is built upon the foundation of the apostles and prophets with Christ as its cornerstone. The risen Lord continues as King of His church, and we have the once-for-all given foundation of the apostles and prophets in the written Word, the Scriptures, in which we hear the voice of Christ speaking with fresh power to each generation of believers in the church. The work of building the church is a divine one: it is God who fits the building together, growing, over time, as God's plan unfolds through the centuries, into a holy temple, a "dwelling of God in the Spirit." It is God's will to join those He draws to His Son to the fellowship of His Son's body, the church. That church then becomes a dwelling place of the Spirit of God, the true fulfillment of the shadow provided by the old covenant temple. It hardly needs to be mentioned that nothing is said about a time when the Holy Spirit would abandon His very dwelling place, a time when believers would no longer be added to the church or that God would Himself destroy it. Given the stability of the foundation, the immovability of the cornerstone, and the wisdom and power of the architect, the idea of the building collapsing on its own is simply ridiculous, so without the explicit statement that God Himself would destroy His own building, passages such as these leave us no reason to believe such a teaching.

■ A Purpose Rarely Mentioned

In a day when the purpose of the church is very much determined in a man-centered fashion, it is rare to hear one of the most important reasons for the church's *visible* and *recognizable* existence emphasized: the demonstration of the wisdom of God. Paul

presented this concept as he continued his explanation of the nature
and purposes of the church:

> To me, the very least of all saints, this grace was given, to
> preach to the Gentiles the unfathomable riches of Christ,
> and to bring to light what is the administration of the mys-
> tery which for ages has been hidden in God who created all
> things; so that the manifold wisdom of God might now be
> made known through the church to the rulers and the au-
> thorities in the heavenly *places* (Ephesians 3:8–10).

Paul considers himself truly blessed to have been given the mission
to preach to the Gentiles the "unfathomable riches of Christ" and to
proclaim his insight into the "administration of the mystery which
for ages has been hidden in God." But in verse 10 Paul speaks of the
church as a *means* of accomplishing something very important:
making known to the "rulers and the authorities in the heavenly
places" the "manifold wisdom of God." The church "makes
known" God's wisdom. Paul does not describe the means by which
this demonstration takes place. Most probably Paul is making reference to the fact of the Jew and Gentile becoming one in the body of
Christ, all through the work of Christ on the cross, applied and
accomplished by the Spirit. But in either case, the church has a role
that is normally ignored: making known God's manifold wisdom to
a watching audience.[1] Was this a one-time demonstration, or is it on
going? There surely is no reason to assume it was a one-time event,
as the text does not point to a time frame in which this demonstration is to take place. The continuing life of the church as it is built
into the final form God intends for it, encompassing all the elect of
God within its walls, is a constant testimony to the manifold wisdom of God. Take away the church, and this demonstration ends.

 This action of making known the manifold wisdom of God is
paralleled a few verses later in one of the high points of the revelation of Scripture regarding the church. As Paul completes a major
section of his letter and prepares to transition into the next subject,
he raises his voice in praise and provides a doxology in these words:

> Now to Him who is able to do far more abundantly beyond
> all that we ask or think, according to the power that works

within us, to Him *be* the glory in the church and in Christ
Jesus to all generations forever and ever. Amen. (Ephesians
3:20–21)

The Apostle speaks of God's great power manifested in the Spirit of
God who works within believers, the very same Spirit that raised
Jesus from the dead. He then ascribes glory to God the Father, "in
the church and in Christ Jesus to all generations." Some translations[2] have "in the church *by* Christ Jesus," but in either case the
same fact is plainly stated: God the Father is to be glorified *in the
church of Jesus Christ* "to all generations." Not to *some* generations, but to *all* generations, forever and ever. The church brings glory to God, for she is His creation. He decreed her existence as surely
as He decreed the salvation of each individual in her number. His
Son made her existence possible by His death, His blood creates her
charter and guarantees her life. Her very existence is an undeniable
proof of the fruit of the death, burial, and resurrection of Jesus
Christ. Her constant testimony to Christ in the celebration of the
Supper, her public remembrance of Him, likewise brings Him glory.
God's will is plainly to glorify Himself through the church, and He
says through His Word that He has no plans to ever cease that demonstration. Now he does so through the visible church's obedience
to Him and the work of the Spirit in building the temple, the dwelling place of the Spirit. And even in eternity to come, the completed
work of God in the church, the Bride of Christ, presented to His Son
spotless in radiant beauty, holy and blameless (Ephesians 5:23) will
continue to bring Him glory.

■ It Bears Repeating
This brief review of only a few of the key passages regarding Christ's
church has raised a number of truths that are directly relevant to the
study we are about to undertake regarding Harold Camping's teachings. In particular:

The church is central to what God is doing in this world.

It is related directly to the proclamation of the gospel,
bearing and safeguarding the truth of the gospel, and providing fellowship for those who embrace the gospel.

There is never any indication that God intends to change His will concerning the church, and in fact, the very opposite is stated.

In the passages that actually address the church directly (in opposition to passages forced into the discussion through a-contextual allegorical interpretation) the Scriptures affirm the *unchanging* intention of God to bring glory to Himself through the church.

God uses the church to make known his manifold wisdom.

Again, there is no indication given that this situation is ever to end, either.

Finally, *the truth that the church is the pillar and foundation of the truth is stated directly in relationship to the local body of believers.*

This cannot be transferred off to a "universal concept."

Before turning to Harold Camping's actual teachings, there is another element of God's truth that must be examined. We live in a day when the church is seen as a consumer product, and "church shopping" is at epidemic proportions. Is it important to be a part of a local church with elders and deacons? The biblical answer is clear.

The Importance and Role
of Church Membership

Harold Camping's teachings about the church come at an inopportune time. That is to say, many are already prone to view the church as they do an automobile, or a house: an item up for sale, something that is bought and sold to the highest bidder. In a day when the church defines itself not by its calling; the holiness of her Master, the privilege and gravity of worship, or the value and power of the precious message entrusted to her, but by the nature of the "audience" she seeks to "draw," it is quite easy to convince the "shoppers" that there is a better show down the road.

Even in "solid" churches there is a very troubling lack of zeal for the church that manifests itself in an unwillingness to be committed to the ministry of service in the local church. For many, "joining the church" is a bothersome activity that is not really important to one's spiritual growth or safety, and for many, it is merely an option, not a command. "Church hopping" is a popular pastime, with many fellowships showing a frightening willingness to cater to such attitudes by putting on a "show" that is guaranteed to "keep the crowds coming." In the process, the gospel is muted and moved to the back shelf, if presented at all.

In the previous chapter we saw that the church is a divine institution, central to God's purposes in this world. We saw that God has willed to redeem an elect people unto Himself, and that this divine work creates the church. The church, truly, is born out of the blood of Calvary (Ephesians 2:13). The act that redeems the individual soul, since it was God's intention thereby to redeem *all* His people, creates, of necessity, the fellowship of the redeemed who are at peace with God and hence at peace with one another as well. Just as we must confess that God had a purpose in the atonement (the redemption of the elect), so too we must see that the church was not merely an after-thought, but part and parcel of the decree of God.

But this is not all the Bible has to say about the church. One of the main biblical truths under attack not only by Mr. Camping, but also by many others is that of church membership. "I don't see the term 'member' in my Bible!" is often the cry. And yet, the teaching of the Bible regarding this issue is both important *and* clear. I shall gladly stand to defend the importance of membership in the local church, and do so on the basis of Scripture itself.

■ God Adds to the Church: A Divine Act

Regeneration is a divine act, accomplished by the Spirit of God at the time and place decreed by God in eternity itself. Just as salvation is God's work, so too God divinely adds *every single person He regenerates* to the body of His Son, the church. This addition is likewise made to the local church as well. Note the record of Luke in Acts 2:41–42, 47:

> So then, those who had received his word were baptized; and that day there were added about three thousand souls. They were continually devoting themselves to the apostles' teaching and to fellowship, to the breaking of bread and to prayer.... [They were] praising God and having favor with all the people. And the Lord was adding to their number day by day those who were being saved.

The most obvious question we must ask is, "added to what?" Obviously, the addition was made to the visible, organized church. In Acts 2:42 those who had been "added" are described as being devoted to the apostles' teaching and to fellowship and to the breaking of bread and to prayer. These are all activities of the organized, gathered body. They could not be devoted to the apostles' teachings if they were not gathered together to hear them teach (1 Timothy 4:13). They could not fellowship alone out in the wilderness of Judea. The breaking of bread took place within the fellowship of believers, and the prayers refer to those of the gathered people of God.

It was to this organized, recognizable, identifiable body of believers that the Lord added daily those who were being saved. This passage does not say that participation in the gathered body was offered to them as an option that would be "best" but unnecessary. It does not say the Lord suggested they would be better off if they joined up. They were added. It is a divine act, just as powerful and efficient as the work of salvation itself.

The rest of the New Testament likewise bears out the continuing validity of these observations. We simply do not find the Word addressing "Lone-Ranger Christians." The over-riding presupposition of the biblical writers is that those to whom they write are part of the fellowship of faith, the church.

One might well point out that the situation has, however, changed since the days of the primitive church in Jerusalem. Today in a major metropolitan area you might have more people in a single city than lived in all of Judea in the ancient context. You also have a proliferation of local church bodies (the reasons for which will be discussed below). But this does not remove the revealed truth that the Lord adds to the church daily those who are being saved. This is part of God's plan.

■ Love One Another

The mark of true Christian discipleship is love for one another (John 13:34–35, 15:12, 17; Romans 12:10; Galatians 5:13; 1 Thessalonians 3:12, 4:9; 1 Peter 1:22, 4:8; 1 John 3:11, 23, 4:7–11). The wide and consistent witness to this divine command in the New Testament shows us how very important it is in God's will for believers.

But it is self-evident that this command has meaning only within the context of Christian fellowship. It is very, very easy to earnestly confess one's love for the brethren from the comfort and ease of one's favorite chair, parked in front of the TV. "Oh yes, I love the brethren!" is easy when we don't have to interact with them, live with them, minister with them, worship with them. It is only when we enter into the fellowship of the church, work together, experience life with all its joys, sorrows, and hardships, in the bond of Christian fellowship, that we learn what it *truly* means to "love one another." This cannot be done in isolation: it assumes we will know whom the "brethren" are that we are to love! And this again points us to the importance of membership in the local church.

■ Elders As Evidence of God's Concern

God has shown his concern for the health, propagation, and perpetuity of the church by establishing it as an ordered body. The church is not an amorphous body without form or design. Instead, we see that the local church is organized with a particular purpose and a particular set of offices that are meant to be self-perpetuating under the guidance and gifting of the Spirit. That is, God has deigned to organize the church with elders and deacons, and He gifts men to fill those offices and hence continue the building and edification of the church. This can be seen throughout the book of Acts, as the church began its mission in the world. For example,

> When they had appointed elders for them in every church, having prayed with fasting, they commended them to the Lord in whom they had believed. (Acts 14:23)

The Apostles, obedient to the Lord's will for them, appointed elders not in *some* churches, but in *every* church. This was part of their work in establishing these churches in the truth. And even after Paul had departed from places such as Ephesus, the eldership continued on, for as Paul traveled toward Jerusalem, he called the elders of that church to him (Acts 20:17). These would be the men that are found faithful and trustworthy to whom Timothy was to pass on Paul's teaching, and to whom the care of the church was to be entrusted (2 Timothy 2:2). Paul said of these men:

> The elders who rule well are to be considered worthy of double honor, especially those who work hard at preaching and teaching. (1 Timothy 5:17)

Elders rule by providing leadership and direction, and as such are due double honor, especially those who labor diligently in the difficult work of preaching and teaching. Obviously, then, God's truth is to be proclaimed and taught as part of the work of the church. This is definitional of the very purpose of the church. And since each new generation of believers needs to be so instructed, the office of elder and the duties attendant to it continues throughout the ministry of the church, as long as there are believers who stand to be edified by that preaching and teaching. This teaching office is so vital the Word repeats the fact that *every* church is to have these elders:

> For this reason I left you in Crete, that you would set in order what remains and appoint elders in every city as I directed you (Titus 1:5).

Appointing elders in the church is part of "setting in order" the affairs of the young church. A church without elders is not in order, biblically speaking. Peter directly addressed the elders of the church, as a fellow elder of the flock:

> Therefore, I exhort the elders among you, as *your* fellow elder and witness of the sufferings of Christ, and a partaker also of the glory that is to be revealed, shepherd the flock of God among you, exercising oversight not under compulsion, but voluntarily, according to *the will of* God; and not for sordid gain, but with eagerness; nor yet as lording it over those allotted to your charge, but proving to be examples to the flock. And when the Chief Shepherd appears, you will receive the unfading crown of glory (1 Peter 5:1–4).

Note that when the Chief Shepherd appears the elders who have served Christ in His church will receive an unfading crown of glory. Never is there any hint of a time when God's people would no longer receive edification through the ministration of elders in the fellowship of the church, and that right up to the point in time when the Lord Himself would "appear."

One of the demonstrations of God's wisdom in the church is the fact that the establishment of the eldership *provides a means of protecting the individual believers placed under their care.* Elders perform a protective service within the body of faith. Immediately above we read the words of Peter to his "fellow elders" exhorting them to undertake their duties with the proper Christ-like attitude. And note the words of Paul to the elders of the church at Ephesus:

> Be on guard for yourselves and for all the flock, among which the Holy Spirit has made you overseers, to shepherd

the church of God which He purchased with His own blood. (Acts 20:28)

The imagery of "being on guard," especially followed as it is in the next verse by reference to "ravenous wolves," speaks of the role of the elders in protecting the flock. Obviously, the person that absents himself or herself from the fellowship of the church no longer has this divinely appointed safeguard. Just as the lone sheep is easy prey for the wolves, so too the lone Christian, separated from the flock, is easy prey for false teachers and every other kind of danger to the soul. God joins the individual sheep to the flock so that shepherds might provide them guidance and protection. *To reject the role of elders in the church is to despise Christ's wisdom and His sovereignty over His church.*

Believers must know, and submit to, those who have been given leadership over them in the fellowship of the church. The writer to the Hebrews commanded his readers to think clearly on this issue:

> Obey your leaders and submit *to them*, for they keep watch over your souls as those who will give an account. Let them do this with joy and not with grief, for this would be un-profitable for you. (Hebrews 13:17)

This command can only be fulfilled when we recognize the necessity of the church, the perpetuity of the church until Christ comes again, and the importance of local church membership. If a person cannot identify who their leaders are, and to whom they are submitting, they are obviously in a state of disobedience to this divine command.

■ The Lord's Supper

To conclude our examination of the importance of church member-ship and God's wisdom in establishing the fellowship of believers, we turn to one of the great joys of the Christian believer's experience of corporate worship: the Lord's Supper. Called "the Eucharist" in ancient writings, most Protestants avoid the term today due to its usage in Roman Catholicism. This is unfortunate, for the term is most expressive: *eucharisteo* in Greek means "to give thanks," and the noun form, *eucharistia*, means "thanksgiving." Paul uses the term when he refers to the Lord Jesus giving "thanks" before breaking the bread (*eucharistesas*), hence its use by ancient writers.

When we look at the biblical teaching about this wonderful ordinance given by the Lord to His church, we learn that it is a celebration of the gathered believers. Paul wrote to the Corinthians about this worship celebration:

> For I received from the Lord that which I also delivered to you, that the Lord Jesus in the night in which He was betrayed took bread; and when He had given thanks, He broke it and said, "This is My body, which is for you; do this in remembrance of Me." In the same way *He took* the cup also after supper, saying, "This cup is the new covenant in My blood; do this, as often as you drink *it*, in remembrance of Me." For as often as you eat this bread and drink the cup, you proclaim the Lord's death until He comes.

Almost every believer has heard these words read prior to the celebration of the Supper. Yet, the English translation does not convey a fact that is often lost on Western-minded, individualistic Christians. Often, when this passage is presented at the Lord's Supper, we hear the last verse, "For as often as you eat this bread and drink the cup, you proclaim the Lord's death until He comes" as a *singular* admonition: that is, we "hear" the "you" as a singular. And while it is surely proper to apply these words to each of us individually (individuals eat the bread and drink the cup, and hence individually engage in the proclamation of the Lord's death), the terms that flowed from Paul's pen were *plurals*. The "you" is a plural pronoun, speaking to the gathered church as a whole.

The Lord Jesus gave His church a way to proclaim His death that is tangible, observable, and to be celebrated "until He comes." All believers are called to proclaim His death in this memorial supper *as part of the gathered body of believers.* And this ordinance is to continue in the church until the Lord comes to take His bride to Himself: it continues as a visible proclamation of the Lord's death until Christ returns to earth.

■ But…There Are So Many Churches!

The primitive model of the church, with a single church in each city, meeting, normally, in a home or from house to house, made joining the "church" a fairly straightforward thing. But we can see even in the writing of the New Testament the rise of heresy and schism. John wrote to a church where there were those who had gone out from the fellowship of the church (1 John 2:18–19), evidently still professing to be Christians, and yet teaching falsehoods. Paul fought heretical movements in many of his letters, most notably in Galatians, where likewise those who opposed and perverted the gospel continued to claim fidelity to Jesus Christ. Peter and Jude, likewise, warned of such things. Obviously, as the church grew, the issue of schism and heresy resulted in a much more complicated state of affairs than existed on the day of Pentecost. The later epistles of the New Testament (2 Peter, Jude, 1, 2 and 3 John) reflect this situation.

Why are there so many churches today? There are two major reasons. First, it is clear that the churches addressed in Scripture were not cookie-cutter clones of one another. The church at Corinth had a different nature to it than the church at Ephesus, or Philippi. Local assemblies have different "chemistries" due to the presence of different mixtures of leaders and people. These differences lead to differences in emphasis. Some congregations have a greater or lesser emphasis upon singing; some a greater or lesser emphasis upon prayer, etc. Some have long services, some shorter. These would be called legitimate differences.

But the major reason for the multiplicity of churches is not merely legitimate differences in style or emphasis: it is due to a failure to apply the divine truth of *Sola Scriptura*. That is, the fundamental reason for doctrinal diversity on key issues is due to the failure to allow Scripture *alone* and *only* to define our faith and practice.[1] We bring our traditions and read them into Scripture, teaching as doctrine the commandments of men. We suffer from ignorance of the whole of Scripture. We have sinful desires that cause us to downplay important and vital commands. And we often pick and choose which portions of the Scriptures we will believe and practice, and which we will simply ignore or bury under a mountain of qualifications.

These issues are related, mainly, to the conservative, vital churches. We do not speak here of those churches and denominations that have replaced the Christian worldview with a secular one, denying the inspiration of the Scriptures, the existence of nonmaterial beings and realities (the supernatural), the existence of miracles, etc. These groups are irrelevant to our discussion, as they are not even a part of the community of faith. While such denominations may have, at one time, held to the Christian worldview, once the foundations of the faith have been abandoned, there is left only a shell, an empty husk. Those who continue, by God's grace, in the faith, should follow the apostolic example and identify those who use the name of Christ and yet deny the faith for what they truly are, so that the world may know the difference between those who follow Christ and those who follow their own hearts and desires in opposition to Christian truth.

Finally, what of the person who says, "I recognize the importance of church membership as seen in the Bible. But there simply is no vital, believing fellowship in my community." There are a number of considerations to be noted in light of the general state of affairs in Western culture today, where admittedly falsehood prevails and the truth, at times, is hard to find.[2]

First, it is possible that in foreign lands, especially those that are predominately Muslim in character, that there would be no organized assembly of believers. In such situations believers should seek, as much as is possible, to avail themselves of fellowship with one another, seeking opportunities of service, if possible. Teaching of the Word through tapes, books, or even the Internet, could be used to assist such believers.

Rarely, though, is the complaint concerning a lack of a "good" church voiced by such people. Those who have experienced life in such situations long for Christian fellowship, and when the opportunity presents itself, they immediately and naturally join in it. Instead, most of those who voice this objection do so on the basis of a *dislike* of the churches that already exist in their area. Such is certainly understandable. There are many fellowships today that do not teach the whole counsel of God. Many are mired in tradition or deeply influenced by "trends" and "movements" that have no basis in biblical revelation. For the soul that loves the truth, constant exposure to a denial of it (even if it is unknowingly done) is very troubling.

Sometimes the issue is simply one of travel. A good, solid church may be an hour or more away. There are many who, due to their strong commitment to truth and the proclamation of the gospel, have driven many hours on the Lord's day so as to be involved in sound churches. Further, many move away from a sound church due to job considerations, and find themselves without a church home. As strange as it sounds in our materialistic culture, might it not be better to place the church above job advancement, so that the availability of a sound church determines whether a promotion would be accepted or not? Many believers have indeed made this commitment, and God has blessed their faithfulness.

The real issue goes to the depth of the desire to grow in the grace and knowledge of the Lord Jesus Christ, and to make use of *all* the means God gives us to do this. Surely one can contemplate any number of circumstances that could make attendance at the stated meetings of the church difficult or even impossible. But the response of the heart of the believer should be to seek every means to overcome these obstacles. Surely there is no biblical defense for those who have no providential hindrance and yet refuse to take their place amongst the people of God. The believer who trusts the message of the gospel as it is found in the pages of Scripture will likewise desire to be obedient to the teaching of those Scriptures regarding the vital necessity of participation in the body of believers, the church.

The Church Age Has Ended?

■ Harold Camping's "New Teaching" Defined

One of the most difficult tasks of God-honoring apologetics is to define with accuracy and integrity the teachings of those groups or individual men to whom we wish to give a biblical and God-honoring response. The difficulty arises simply because one is often faced with a "moving target," especially when the group or person believes in or practices some kind of "new revelation." Mormonism, for example, claims the ability to receive "latter-day revelation," so that LDS leaders are actually viewed as apostles of Christ, capable of speaking with the authority of Paul or John of old. And even when a group denies direct or continuing revelation, like the Watchtower Bible and Tract Society (Jehovah's Witnesses), in *practice* the leadership of the organization becomes an authority alongside the Bible or *above* the Bible. The interpretation of the leader or group becomes the final authority, leading to ever-changing beliefs and interpretations.

Harold Camping's teachings are in a similar state of flux at any one point. As most readers know, Mr. Camping is well known for having predicted the coming of Christ in 1994. In the period leading up to 1994 his teachings, including the passages in which he found clear evidence in support of his position, changed and grew in number. New spiritual "insights" were gained as well, so that a person who sought to respond to his teaching would have a hard time being perfectly "up to date" until after the events of 1994 were completed.

The same situation is faced today with his new teaching concerning the church. Each passing week brings a new "insight," a new spiritual understanding that had not been "seen" before. This makes his position somewhat of a moving target, as it grows and develops with time.

Despite these considerations, it is possible to accurately and fairly represent Camping's teaching, as it exists at the time of this writing. As many people are greatly confused by his teachings, we must first condense them down to an understandable summary before looking at the particulars of his argumentation.

■ The Church Age Has Ended

The most basic element of Camping's new teaching is quite simple: according to him, the church of Jesus Christ, as it finds expression in local, organized bodies, no longer exists. There are no more local churches, no elders, pastors, or deacons. There is no more Lord's Supper, no more Christian baptism. The visible church has been judged, destroyed, ended. It is no more.

The rest of his teaching flows from this basic premise. Most of his time is spent in defense of the assertion through unique, never-before-seen interpretations of the Bible. Indeed, he admits openly that no one before him has ever understood the *real* meaning of passages such as John 21 (the major basis of his current teaching).

Based upon his unique interpretations, Camping teaches that from the beginning of the church age (which he believes existed for 1900 years) the church has been imperfect, just as the nation of Israel had been imperfect. He speaks of the existence of "high places" in the history of Israel, places of idolatrous worship that plagued the people of Israel. Camping notes that God blessed many of the Israelite kings even though they did not get rid of all of the high places in Israel. Camping asserts that the existence of the high places in the history of Israel is parallel to the existence of false doctrines in the confessions of the church. These "high places" constitute false teachings that come solely from the minds of men, and not from the Bible. It is important to note what Camping believes constitutes these "high places." He has been fairly consistent over time in producing the same list of alleged false teachings at this point:

1. Women pastors.[1]
2. Universal atonement.[2]
3. Baptismal regeneration.[3]
4. Faith as an instrument of salvation.[4]
5. A future millennium.[5]
6. Divorce for fornication.[6]

After listing these things, for example, Camping says, "But these are high places, in that they have come from the exalted minds of men instead of coming from God."[7] It is immediately evident that Camping is not addressing the wide range of liberal churches that deny the inspiration of Scripture, the existence of miracles, the resurrection or the deity of Christ. His comments are directed toward conservative, evangelical, even Reformed churches, for he speaks of their confessions of faith as enshrining these "high places," and non-Reformed churches are not known for their use of confessions. It is hardly surprising that the largest portion of Harold Camping's followers are drawn from just these conservative, evangelical, Reformed congregations.

Camping believes these "high places" have existed in the church throughout the 1900 years of its history. But, just as God eventually brought judgment upon Israel for idolatry, so too God has brought judgment to bear upon the church for her unwillingness to remove the high places.

Drawing heavily from highly questionable allegorical interpretations of the book of Revelation and John 21, Camping teaches that after 1900 years of church history, God allowed Satan to destroy the church. To use his terms, God "took away the candlestick" from the churches. There are two important results of this action on God's part:

First, the Holy Spirit is no longer active in the organized churches. He is no longer there to apply the preached word, so that even if the gospel is rightly proclaimed, the Spirit does not bless it.

Second, as a result, *no one is being saved in the formal churches any longer.* Camping emphasizes this quite heavily. He insists that multitudes are still being saved, but they are hearing the gospel not from the churches, but from Family Radio, his own ministry.[8] All supposed conversions within the church in this day and age are false: no person can possibly be saved where the Holy Spirit is no longer active.

This claim is so outrageous it needs to be repeated and considered in-depth. The means God has used to evangelize the world (the role of the church in bringing glory to God, and all the other things the church does that are mentioned in Scripture, are, by and large, ignored by Camping in his teachings on this subject), while still existing externally, has actually been destroyed. Camping says the two witnesses in Revelation 11:7–8 who are killed represent the church, and since they are slain, then the church on earth likewise can be destroyed.[9] Elsewhere he draws an elaborate allegorical interpretation from the text of John 21 and the account of Jesus' appearance to the disciples while they are fishing. He focuses upon the appearance of a "boat" in John 21, asserting that boats represent the church. Noting that in Luke 5:7 two boats (Camping also indicates that the number "two" is relevant to the church, but upon what basis he asserts this one can only guess) began to sink, so great was the catch of fish, Camping insists that we understand that the church can "sink" and be destroyed because of this. He then moves this concept into the text of John 21 (without providing any meaningful reason for so doing) and makes the boat in which the Apostles are fishing a picture of the church. Since they are unable to bring the net containing the great catch of fish into the boat, this, we are told, speaks to the time when the church will not be able to bring in those who are being saved. They are saved "outside" the boat, i.e., outside the church.

Of course, Harold Camping is not ignorant of the *content* of the Scriptures, and he is well aware of the passages in the Bible that speak of the continuity or perpetuity of the church. Passages such as Matthew 16:18 (Jesus' promise to build His church) and Ephesians 3:20–21 are well known to him. He replies to these passages by making reference to the distinction between the eternal/invisible church and the earthly/visible church seen in local congregations. He assures us that the eternal church is, in fact, indestructible because it is made up solely of the redeemed and they cannot lose their salvation. This eternal church is heavenly in nature, and cannot be destroyed. We have already examined this concept in the preceding chapter and have seen that it does not provide Mr. Camping any grounds for his teaching, for the church, in God's providence, exists as an organized body with elders and deacons, the ordinances, and the ministry of worship, demonstration of God's wisdom, and the proclamation of the gospel. These functions demand the existence of the visible, organized church made up of local congregations, not merely of an invisible, heavenly body.

Camping rightly recognizes that the Bible presents the ordinances of the Lord's Supper and Baptism as *church* activities. They are given to the church, not to any other body. He is therefore consistent in teaching that since the church age has ended, so too there is no longer any availability of these ordinances. Christian baptism has ended from his perspective. New converts need not be baptized in obedience to Christ's command, an amazing anomaly when one considers it, for while Camping still believes the Great Commission must be pursued, a portion of that command has now been rescinded ("baptizing them"). New believers in Jesus Christ are to be denied this wonderful testimony of faith in Jesus Christ.

Likewise, Christians can no longer celebrate the Supper. While they can read about it in the text of Scripture, and receive "edification" as a result, they themselves cannot partake of the ordinance even when they gather with fellow believers in "fellowships." It is an ecclesiastical ordinance and therefore cannot continue when God has destroyed the church.

■ Do Not Forsake the Fellowship

Ironically, Camping insists that a number of commands found in the New Testament in the context of the church continue in force today. Of course, he denies the connection to the church (without any meaningful basis for doing so). For example, he often reminds people of the command of Hebrews 10:23–25,

> Let us hold fast the confession of our hope without wavering, for He who promised is faithful; and let us consider how to stimulate one another to love and good deeds, not forsaking our own assembling together, as is the habit of some, but encouraging *one another*; and all the more as you see the day drawing near.

In the original context this referred, of course, to gathering together in the church (cf. Heb. 13:17). But despite this glaring fact, Camping emphasizes the necessity of continuing to gather together today, despite the destruction of the church. He encourages his followers, then, to find like-minded believers with whom they can fellowship on the Sunday Sabbath. If they cannot find such a fellowship (they are few and far between), they should gather with family and sing hymns and pray and, of course, listen to Family Radio and Harold Camping.

It is painfully obvious that at this point in time Mr. Camping has no real idea how to handle all the practical questions that flow from this sudden shift from "church" to "fellowship." Though he actually encourages entire churches to de-constitute themselves as churches and adopt the term "fellowship" (a process that would include removing all elders and deacons, a process Mr. Camping has brought about in the church where he served as an elder for many years), he cannot tell these "fellowships" how they are to work. For example, a caller to the Open Forum asked if it was now acceptable to have women address the fellowships as "preachers." His answer was no, 1 Timothy 2 is still in force (though again, that passage is in reference to the church). Questions concerning marriages, burials, and all sorts of other "mundane" issues about these "fellowships" have yet to receive any answer outside of Harold Camping's "suggestions." The reason is simple: the Word of God knows nothing about elderless, deaconless, leaderless, unorganized "fellowships"

■ Flee the Churches

Finally, though he did not at first emphasize this element, Camping now strongly teaches that we are to flee the churches. Christians should not desire to stay in a dead structure that has been judged by God and destroyed, especially since the Holy Spirit is no longer active there. Drawing from another allegorical interpretation of Scripture, Camping interprets the command to flee from Jerusalem when it is surrounded by enemies as a command to leave the church once it is destroyed by God (Luke 21:20–21). This element was not present when Camping first began to teach that the church age was ended (though, of course, many saw it as the logical conclusion of the teaching).

Obviously, this is the teaching that has now started to attract more widespread attention. It was one thing to say the church had ended. It is another to start telling your followers to leave the churches they have been in for years or decades. This is especially true given the fact that Family Radio had, for decades, partnered with local churches, airing the worship services of many congregations. Camping has decreed that this should end, and that anyone who speaks on the station should avoid mention of the church, should not give meeting times for churches, and should not call themselves a pastor. Obviously, the vast majority of those congregations that once aired their programs on Family Radio have ceased to do so.

And so in broad outline these are the issues that have prompted this response. We have already listened to the Word's teaching about the church, its perpetuity, and its purposes. Let us now turn to the heart of his error: his use of constant allegorical interpretation.

Hearing God Accurately

■ The Interpretation of Scripture

Without any controversy, the central issues raised by the teachings of Harold Camping regarding the church and the end of the age are issues of interpretation. No one has ever taught what Harold Camping is now teaching in the form he presents it. Surely, many have taught that the church had lost its authority or life in the past: but the key fact regarding Camping's teaching is that he derives his teaching from what he calls the "spiritual meaning" of the biblical text. As we have seen the constant element of Camping's teaching is the non-contextual assertion, "And we see that this represents the church" or "We know that the number two is significant" or "When we see this term we know it must represent this." Camping's allegorical interpretation is the heart and soul of his teaching and the source of the zeal of his followers as well. But is this kind of spiritual allegorization of *the entirety* of Scripture a valid procedure? Or has Harold Camping fallen into the standard path of all false teachers of the past, using the Scriptures as a pre-text for his own doctrines and teachings?

■ Rightly Handling the Word of God

How shall we approach the text of Scripture? Such has been a source of debate from the beginning. Indeed, it is not a debate limited to the Christian faith: any religious system that asserts that God has communicated in a written form to His creature man must deal with the fact that written language is capable, in more or less valid ways, of different kinds of interpretation.[1] Part of this is due to the fact that written sources can take different literary forms. We find in Scripture such forms as prophecy, apocalyptic, didactic, poetic, and parabolic (parables). These different forms require different sets of interpretation to make sense.

However, it has been the conclusion of the large majority of scholars since the time of the Reformation that the first and foremost element of interpreting Scripture (and indeed any historical document) is to first and primarily determine *the meaning and intention of the author in his own native context.* That is, the first job of the interpreter is to discover what *the author* intended to communicate *when he wrote* and how this would have been understood *by the audience the author intended to address.* How we do this with different kinds of literature we will consider below. For now, however, it is vital to establish this first rule of meaningful interpretation, for if this rule is established, the entirety of Mr. Camping's teaching is refuted, for the primary essence of his allegorical form of interpretation is that the original meaning of the original author in its original context is *not* the meaning we are to be concerned about. There is, allegedly, a "higher" meaning that is available only to those who have access to the special "knowledge" that allows them to see past the basic, mundane meaning.

The foundation of sound biblical hermeneutics in the determination of the original meaning of the biblical text can be established by the consideration of how we interpret *any* written language. This can be illustrated by noting that Mr. Camping has put his own views into writing and, of course, his teachings exist in recorded form which are capable likewise of being transcribed and interpreted. By what rules would Mr. Camping wish to have his own writings interpreted? Would Mr. Camping desire to allow you to use allegorical interpretation on his *own* writings and teachings? For example, Mr. Camping asserted:

> We read in verse 4, Jesus stood on the shore, but the disciples knew not that it was Jesus. Now that's a very negative statement, because this is a picture of the church, and somehow they're not recognizing Jesus. There's a major defect in their understanding of what Jesus is doing, what Jesus' program is.[2]

Let us first apply sound principles of interpretation to this passage. Mr. Camping is talking about the end of the church age as he interprets it. He is drawing from John chapter 21, verse 4, which then determines the context in which we are to read his comments. He is speaking of Jesus in His post-resurrection appearance to His disciples that is recorded in John 21. Mr. Camping understands the statement that the apostles did not know it was Jesus standing on the shore as a negative thing, for he believes the apostles as a group are acting as a picture of the church in this passage. He believes this means that in this particular "picture" the church is not recognizing Jesus as it should. He believes that this picture presents to us a "major defect" in the understanding of the church as to what Jesus is doing at this point in history. They do not understand what Jesus' program is.

But now let us ignore the basic elements of interpretation and see what we can "find" in this same passage from Mr. Camping. What is *really* being said here? Well, based upon my study and my spiritual insights, I understand Mr. Camping to be addressing Family Radio. When he says that Jesus is standing on the seashore, we know the seashore is made of sand, and often the world's population is represented as the "sand of the sea." So, this is referring to a time when Jesus stands over the entire population of the earth, reigning as King. This refers to the time when the gospel of the kingdom is being preached across the world, of course, and the gospel is preached in the church, Christ's body, where He reigns as King. So the time frame the Word is referring to is the time when God grants success to His church. The disciples represent the leadership of Family Radio, for, of course, they are in a boat fishing. Family Radio has always sought to be fishers of men, so obviously the Word of God is telling us that here the Apostles are a picture of the board of Family Radio who continue to attempt to win souls (the fish). But there is a problem. They do not recognize Jesus standing as King in His church over the population of the world. They are ignorant of the close connection between Jesus and His church, and as such, they remain "separated" from him, trying, in vain, to gather souls outside of the God-ordained means that we see so clearly here in the Bible.

Now we can immediately see that applying different kinds of interpretation results in diametrically opposite interpretations. And while I can argue that the understandings I presented in my allegorical, spiritual "interpretation" of Camping's words are, in fact, consistent with biblical truths, I cannot logically or rationally argue that *the interpretation itself represents Mr. Camping's actual intended teaching*. My *conclusions* may be accurate, but they are not true to the basis from which I drew them.

This is why we must engage in meaningful hermeneutics, the science of accurately, fairly, and logically reading the words of someone else so as to actually allow them to speak for themselves. This is why we pay so much attention to the work of *exegesis*, the reading *out of the text* its true meaning (the opposite of which is *eisegesis*, the reading *into* the text of a meaning its original author never intended): if we do not *exegete* a text, we have no right to claim the authority of the text itself, for we are not *listening* to the text. We are talking and hoping to insert our thoughts into the written word. It is obvious that Mr. Camping would not accept my "interpretation" of his words. He would rightly be frustrated at such a consistent effort on my part to ignore his own context and meaning. And yet, *the unique elements of Camping's teachings* are uniformly derived from this very same kind of non-contextual, allegorical interpretation that he would never allow anyone to use on his own writings and teachings. The inconsistency is striking.

■ Grammatical-Historical Exegesis

To exegete any written text is to *read out* of its words the meaning that is expressed by those words, phrases, clauses, sentences, paragraphs, etc. The opposite of exegesis is *eisegesis,* which involves *reading into* the written text a meaning that is not derived from the words, their grammatical form, their relationship to other words (called "syntax"), their context, etc.

Of course, many balk at the idea of applying the same rules of interpretation to the Bible that we use to read any written document. Strong sermons can be preached about the unique nature of Scripture, with the idea being communicated clearly that if we do not adopt some "spiritual" means of interpretation we are somehow denigrating the inspired nature of Scripture itself. Should we not treat the text of Scripture differently than we would the text of Plato or Homer or other works of antiquity?

The argument truly misses the point, and that badly. The point is not how we interpret the languages spoken in the past, hence, the text itself. The question is how we *understand* the result of that act of interpretation. That is, documents written in human language require us to interpret them as they were written, whether they are inspired documents or not. But it is what we do with the results of that interpretation that matters. The "spiritual nature" of how we interpret the Bible comes from our conviction of its nature as divine revelation. As a result, we do not interpret the Word while entertaining the idea that what we are reading can be self-contradictory or untrue. If we interpret passages in such a way as to render the Scriptures self-contradictory, we have obviously missed the author's meaning (or, more likely, have assumed a meaning that is in error).

The issue here is not, "Is there more to the Scriptures than mere human words?" All Christians gladly confess this. Surely there is a spiritual, living dimension to the Word. We truly must separate the *method of determining the intended meaning of the author* from other issues such as, "Is the meaning of the author in his own time and own context the *only* possible meaning that is legitimate" or "Does it not take a work of the Spirit in the heart to cause a person to understand *and obey* the Word out of love for God?" These are "later" issues, for they assume that we can first determine a basis upon which to answer such questions, and that basis is the intended teaching of the Scriptures themselves.

Since many believers are introduced to the study of the Scriptures "higher up the ladder" so to speak, the more basic issues of the *how* of interpretation are often left unspoken and assumed. Most churches do not seek to introduce their members to "hermeneutics" or "exegesis" or such related fields of study, resulting in a basic ignorance of the issues faced in interpreting the text of Scripture itself. At times, the method of exegesis popular in a particular group is a "given," part of the very "tradition" of that group, and is never discussed or examined for consistency. Indeed, some groups identify the entire pursuit of a consistent hermeneutic as an "attack" upon "the faith" for no other reason than that the core beliefs that set them apart are not the result of sound exegesis but of special pleading.

The grammatical-historical method of interpretation is a means of guaranteeing that we are hearing what the text says, not what we *want* the text to say. This is a vitally important point, especially when it comes to the Scriptures. When reading secular texts we are not nearly as tempted to insert a foreign meaning into the words of the author, since it is rare that such a text would be given sufficient importance to warrant the effort. We "naturally" apply sound rules of interpretation to such documents since we are not at all threatened by the results. But when it comes to the text of the Bible, much more is at stake. But if we are consistent in our beliefs, and *truly* want to hear what the Scriptures are saying and not what we *want* them to say or *feel* they should say, we need to have a means of reading the text that does not allow us to "slip" our own thoughts into the text under the guise of "interpretation." The Bible needs to say the same thing in each language, in each culture, in each context, or it cannot be the means of communicating the truth to us that Christians believe it to be. The grammatical-historical method allows us to be both honest and consistent with the text of the Bible.

Many fine works exist on the subject of biblical interpretation, hermeneutics, or exegesis, and it is beyond the scope of this work to repeat what they have to say.[3] Instead, a basic outline will be provided with special emphasis upon the issues that are important regarding Harold Camping's teachings, and especially his constant use of allegorical interpretation as the basis of his "insights."

■ Grammatical

The first term in "grammatical-historical" refers to the actual meaning of the words as they are used in the original languages. The Old Testament was written in the Hebrew tongue, with a smattering of Aramaic (a related language) in later books. The New Testament was written in Greek.[4] These are the languages God chose for the giving of His revelation. To engage in in-depth exegesis of the text requires that we look carefully at what the original authors wrote, in the language they used. While English translations are fine for reading and most needed forms of study, exegesis has always required the use of the original tongues.[5] Anyone wishing to closely study the writings of Plato will likewise need to learn classical Greek; the writings of Plutarch, Latin; the works of Pascal, French, etc.

We often differentiate between various aspects of the study that is subsumed under the word "grammatical." For our purposes, we will discuss two aspects under this term, the first being the *meaning* of the word, the second being the *grammatical form* of the word.

When we speak of the meaning of a word, we often think of looking up a word in a dictionary and getting a static meaning. But obviously that is a simplistic way of looking at it. Words have a range of meaning (called a "semantic range"), and any particular use of a word intends to locate its meaning somewhere within that range. Other elements of the language will determine where in the range of meaning the author intends the word to be placed (contextual issues such as grammar and subject under discussion, for example). But especially when examining ancient texts in foreign languages, the first task is to determine basic meaning.

The past number of generations has seen an explosion in our knowledge of the backgrounds of the languages of the Bible, and a corresponding expansion in our knowledge of the ways in which terms which appear in the text of sacred scripture were used in secular settings. We have uncovered the records of ancient nations that surrounded Israel and used similar languages and terminology, greatly increasing our ability to place particular words within a wider range of uses, leading to a better understanding of their meaning. The discovery of a great cache of secular writings contemporaneous to the writing of the New Testament has likewise provided us with a much deeper understanding of the context and vocabulary of the apostolic writings.

Since we cannot simply pick up a "Greek dictionary" published in the days of Christ, we must create the modern equivalent by diligent study of the resources available to us. Modern lexicons of the ancient languages are based upon centuries of such study.

One of the most common errors made by beginning interpreters of the biblical text is the assumption that the meaning of any particular word remains constant throughout the biblical text. This is transparently not the case. Different authors may use a particular term in different ways, one emphasizing one aspect of its meaning, another emphasizing a different "shade" of its meaning. The "wider" the range of meaning a word can carry; the more likely one will find it being used in a variety of ways. For example, in John 1:1 we read about "the Word." The Greek term, *logos*, is a word that has a very wide semantic domain. Its basic meaning is "word," but it can be used in many other ways. It can mean message, talk, conversation, question, charge, matter, thing, reason, basis, or account, all depending on the context in which it is used. Trying to force a single meaning on the word is not only unwise; it would result in utter gibberish in some instances. For example, in Matthew 5:32 Jesus says, "but I say to you that everyone who divorces his wife, except for *the* reason (Greek: *logos*) of unchastity, makes her commit adultery." If we tried to make *logos* mean "word" in every instance, we could not make sense of this passage at all.

Words do not exist in isolation from each other. When we speak, we place them in relationship to other words. When we put a word in a particular form (or in some languages, a particular position in a phrase or sentence as well), we do so for a reason. The forms of language communicate meaning. An illustration might be useful at this point. In John 4:2 we read, "although Jesus Himself was not baptizing, but His disciples were." I once had a member of the LDS Church posit the idea that the actual meaning of this text was, "Jesus Himself was not baptizing anyone but His disciples," the idea being that Jesus did, in fact, baptize His disciples (this would be helpful to the LDS concept of authority and baptism). In replying to him, I examined the text and pointed out that the phrase "the disciples" is in the nominative case in the original language. If "the disciples" were the direct object of the verb "to baptize," it would not appear in the nominative (the case of the subject) but in the accusative (the case of the direct object). The individual accepted this explanation with thanks. When John penned those words under the guidance and direction of the Holy Spirit, part of that divine revelation involved the determination of the very form of the phrase "the disciples." The nominative case communicates part of the meaning, and to ignore that case is to ignore the intention of John in writing the text as he did. *Any interpretation that does not allow the author to communicate meaning in this fashion by ignoring these elements is not interpretation at all.*

■ Historical

Under this subject fall a number of vital elements in proper interpretation of a text. Most of these topics are part of the all important term "context." Almost every interpretational issue revolves around properly understanding the context. Some of the major elements of the "context" include:

Immediate context. This includes the relationship of words to one another (syntax), to clauses, sentences, and paragraphs. The immediate context is normally that which is the most closely scrutinized. But when making decisions about the meaning of terms, for example, often broader contextual issues come into play.

Wider context. This would refer to those issues extending from major divisions of a book (such as one of the Gospels) or an epistle (such as Romans) to the context of an individual author (Paul's writings as a whole, or John's epistles). For example, when reading an extended argument, such as that presented in Romans, the flow of the argument, the cogency of the position, the goal to which the author is pressing, all must be taken into consideration in the interpretation of individual passages. When we interpret an author in such a way as to make him contradict himself, we have probably missed his meaning. When we understand him in such a fashion as to turn his own argument upon its head, we have likewise probably misinterpreted him. *Authorial context* would refer to those issues that arise from looking at the writings of a single author. Most commonly, given the nature of the New Testament, this involves examining Paul's writings as a body, seeing how he uses terms, communicates similar ideas in various letters, repeats themes, etc. The more we have from an author, the more we can determine his "style." This is certainly the case with Paul, and likewise Luke and John provide us with a large enough body of writing to get a good firm hold on their "style."

A vital part of accurate interpretation involves recognizing the *kind* of writing one is interpreting. That is, one does not interpret a parable in the exact same way as apocalyptic material, or teaching (didactic), or historical narrative, or poetry. This is an area of common failure in biblical exegesis. Apocalyptic literature, for example, *by nature* utilizes symbols and representations and metaphors. Didactic teaching, *by nature*, does not. Determining the actual *intention* of the original author in these situations requires close attention to the means they are using to communicate their point. The *literal* meaning of a passage may *not* be the obvious meaning *if the style being used demands otherwise.* Interpreting parables as if they are historical narrative, for example, will lead to errors. But interpreting a parable properly will lead to a *literal* meaning that goes beyond the simple words on the page.

The historical backgrounds of the books of the Bible are likewise vitally important. When reading the gospels, for example, the background of first century Judea and Judaism provides us with incredibly important grounds upon which to interpret the words of Jesus. The more we know about the historical context from which an author wrote the more firm we can be in our grasp of his meaning and purpose. Anyone who engages in writing today, whether it is of a book, article, or just a letter, realizes that misunderstandings can arise if the context from which the work is written is ignored. Passing references that make perfect sense within the context of the writer, if they are unknown to a later reader, may be misconstrued or misinterpreted.

For example, the terrorist attacks upon the United States that took place on September 11, 2001, have impacted the lives of everyone living in North America. Much of what is written today in personal correspondence will make reference to these events. We may write an email to a relative and make reference to having difficulty making a particular flight "because of security." We might refer to concerns someone has about "some strange people living next door." Without the context of the September 11 attacks, these words may be misunderstood, and any number of false conclusions drawn as a result. Jesus made reference to a contemporary event in just this fashion:

> Or do you suppose that those eighteen on whom the tower
> in Siloam fell and killed them were *worse* culprits than all
> the men who live in Jerusalem? (Luke 13:4)

Here the Lord uses a contemporary event to illustrate a point. The more we know about these events and the general context of the day the more accurately we can understand the message being communicated by the text.

When we ignore issues of context we are showing a fundamental disrespect to the text itself. None of us would wish our letters or correspondence to be read by future generations in such a fashion. Surely, then, we must put forth the effort to understand the words of Scripture in such a fashion that we are not merely inserting our own fancies or desires into the words of others, but are, instead, truly "listening" to what was originally intended.

■ What Is Wrong with Allegorical Interpretation?

There are many means of interpretation that are fundamentally contradictory to the grammatical-historical method of interpretation. For our purposes, the main method we need to examine is the allegorical method. Allegorical interpretation is based upon the idea that the basic meaning communicated by the text is *not* the "real" meaning. Instead, there are other meanings. This view, popularized especially by the Egyptian writer Origen in the late second and early third centuries, begins with the assumption that the plain meaning cannot possibly be the most important, since "anyone can understand it." If a non-Christian can understand it, it must not be "it." So, he also taught that there was a second meaning, a moral meaning, which requires more insight to understand. But even this was not enough. The "true" meaning of the text was the "spiritual" meaning. This is a meaning hidden from the view of the unenlightened. It requires "spiritual insight" to see. And it is not derived from examining context or grammar or syntax or anything else. It is derived from "seeing" things in the text, "discovering" that this person is a picture of another, this object "represents" another, etc.

The fundamental reason we must reject allegorical interpretation of the biblical text is really quite simple: it is unverifiable. That is, there is no possible way to determine that the results of using allegorical methodology have anything whatsoever to do with the actual meaning of the text. One man's allegorical understanding can have no compelling force upon the thinking of another, for that person may well "see" something completely different in the text. Since the means provided by human language to communicate meaning are by-passed in the allegorical method, there are no "safety nets" to keep one from wandering off into the most fanciful of "interpretations" of the text. Hence, the person who says "the allegorical meaning of this text is such and so" cannot claim the actual authority of the text for his interpretation, for the actual source of the interpretation is not the text itself but the mind of the interpreter. This is why we say there can be no compelling force to one's allegorical interpretation, for it is merely personal, and if anyone else accepts it, it is because they choose to trust the *allegorical interpreter* rather than the *text itself*. Allegorical interpretations can have no more authority than the one proclaiming them.

When applied to the biblical text this methodology is devastating. The authority of the text is destroyed. No allegorical interpreter can honestly say, "The Word of God says," for in reality, the Word of God has been replaced with the more or less fanciful thoughts of the interpreter himself. The Christian doctrine of inspiration sets the Christian Scriptures apart from all other claimed divine revelations in that Christians believe the Scriptures are God-breathed. This means the written word communicates to us infallibly the very speaking of God in a miraculously personal manner (Matthew 22:31). The authority of the Word is not based upon *the interpreter* but upon the *inspired text* itself. The message of the written Word is the same through the course of time.[6] Without this affirmation, the Word becomes a purely subjective document, incapable of communicating divine truth with certainty.

This point cannot be over-emphasized. *Allegorical interpretation destroys biblical authority.* It replaces the divine message with the imaginations of the interpreter, and as such opens the door wide for every kind of abuse of the text. False teachers, seeking to draw away disciples after themselves (Acts 20:30), utilize such means to release themselves from the unchanging standards of God's Word and insert, under the guise of "thus sayeth the Lord," their own pet doctrines and teachings. The Christian who is untaught and unstable, a novice in the Word, can easily be taken in by such a teacher who exudes confidence and often hides the false teachings behind a veneer of self-professed orthodoxy. So when we defend proper exegetical methodology, we are not merely arguing about tangential issues, we are, in reality, defending the very authority of the Word, and its ability to speak with clarity and force to each generation and in every place.

■ But What About Galatians 4?

But those who use the allegorical method are not without their defenses. The most obvious counter-argument that could be offered is to refer to the following passage from the Apostle Paul:

> Tell me, you who want to be under law, do you not listen to the law? For it is written that Abraham had two sons, one by the bondwoman and one by the free woman. But the son by the bondwoman was born according to the flesh, and the

son by the free woman through the promise. This is allegorically speaking, for these *women* are two covenants: one
proceeding from Mount Sinai bearing children who are to
be slaves; she is Hagar. Now this Hagar is Mount Sinai in
Arabia and corresponds to the present Jerusalem, for she is
in slavery with her children. But the Jerusalem above is free;
she is our mother. For it is written, *"Rejoice, barren woman
who does not bear; break forth and shout, you who are not
in labor; for more numerous are the children of the desolate
than of the one who has a husband."* And you brethren, like
Isaac, are children of promise. But as at that time he who
was born according to the flesh persecuted him *who was
born* according to the Spirit, so it is now also. But what does
the Scripture say? *"Cast out the bondwoman and her son,
for the son of the bondwoman shall not be an heir with the
son of the free woman."* So then, brethren, we are not children of a bondwoman, but of the free woman. (Galatians
4:21–31)

The relevance is immediately obvious: in illustrating his point Paul
refers to two Old Testament characters, Sarah and Hagar, the free-
woman and the bondwoman. He introduces them and then says in
verse 24, "This is allegorically speaking, for these women are two
covenants." In fact, our English term "allegory" is merely a trans-
literation of the very Greek term used, *allegoreo.* The New King
James renders the same word as "symbolic." This is the only place
the word appears in the Bible (either in the New Testament or in the
Greek Septuagint translation of the Old). In either case, here an
inspired Apostle makes a point from the law based upon seeing a
symbolic, allegorical meaning in the text. Does this not negate
everything we just said?

   There are a number of problems in citing this passage in support
of the kind of allegorical interpretation practiced by Camping. First,
Paul was not in any way suggesting that the actual historical texts
that deal with Sarah and Hagar are, in fact, irrelevant and unwor-
thy of being taken at face value and understood in a grammatical–
historical method. Of course, Paul himself interpreted those very
same texts in a very literal, very grammatical-historical means in
Romans and in Galatians (see, for example, his use of Genesis 15:6

and the act of faith on Abraham's part, which Paul places firmly in the context of history itself in Romans 4:9ff). Paul would be very inconsistent with himself if, in fact, he were to take sections of the Genesis narrative and interpret them literally in one place, and then allegorically in another.

Next, it is very important to note that Paul is giving us an illustration here. He has established the facts of his teaching by direct teaching and by direct use of the Old Testament Scriptures. In Galatians chapter three Paul had brought in numerous Scriptures without once resorting to an allegorical interpretation of them. They were passages directly relevant to the point he was making *on the grammatical-historical* level. Indeed, he even belabors the point in 3:16 regarding the difference between a singular and a plural use of a word (seed vs. seeds). The illustration offered in chapter four, then, does not form the foundation of his argument, but instead illustrates one point of it. That point has to do with bondage and freedom, and Hagar, a bondwoman, becomes an excellent example by which to contrast the two covenants, one that brings bondage, the other which brings freedom. The apostle has already presented the contrast directly, now he gives what might be called a "sermon illustration" from a well known fact of biblical history that would "speak" to those he is addressing. In the teaching immediately prior to the allegorical story the constant theme is freedom versus bondage, and he finally addresses those who seek to be "under the law" (v. 21) by use of an allegorical story *from* the law. He draws this story from their common belief in the law as a divine revelation, and presses the same contrast of bond/free, law/promise. The point here is that Paul does not begin his defense with an allegory, he illustrates an already established truth by it.

Further, while it may seem rather obvious, Paul is here giving us the same kind of spiritual insight the writer to the Hebrews provides, under the leadership of the Holy Spirit. This is inspired material, and outside of cult leaders and the like, interpreters of the Word today do not stand in the Apostle's position. God has revealed that it was His intention to place in the law and in the ceremonies of the Old Covenant a picture of the coming fulfillment, the Messiah, Jesus Christ. Paul taught that what had been written was for our encouragement and edification (Romans 15:4). The same Spirit who was guiding Paul as he wrote to the Galatians guided Moses as he wrote

Genesis. Hence, this places this inspired commentary and illustration outside the context of asking how we today, who are not writing Scripture, are to understand what was written. While we have the same Spirit, the Spirit is not performing the same miraculous work in us in *revelation* that He did in Paul or Moses. He is not giving new revelation, but is instead active in enlightening our minds, not to see hidden meanings never before seen, but to understand, and apply, the truth that has been forever recorded in Scripture. The Spirit led Paul to make a handful of symbolic, allegorical applications of truths he had already taught from Scripture (another example might be that of the "rock" that followed Israel being Christ, 1 Corinthians 10:4). To expand this divine action into a mandate to apply the allegorical method of interpretation to Scripture is unwarranted. And as we shall see, Mr. Camping's allegorical interpretation goes far beyond anything Paul ever dreamed of using or producing.

Should the argument be expanded to the types and shadows placed by God in the Old Covenant to point us to the fulfillment in the New, we would likewise reply by stating that such is not a warrant for engaging in allegorical interpretation of the text of Scripture. God divinely placed these types in the ordinances of sacrifice and worship that he enjoined upon the Jewish people. It is their *nature* to function in that fashion. Not everything is a type or shadow, and this is the great error of allegorical interpretation that goes beyond types and shadows provided by God Himself: not everything in the Bible is meant to be a container for some "hidden meaning." "Thou shalt not murder" means exactly what it says. We may be able to expand upon this, discuss how we should honor and protect life, and make application in any number of areas. But the meaning of the text is clear and unambiguous. When we attempt to say that the "real" meaning is found in assigning some separate meaning to the text, seeing in "murder" a picture of something else, something related to current events in our day or a movement in our culture, then we are surely replacing the original intent with our own. This comes to full fruition in the allegorical interpretations of Harold Camping, which abandon any and all connection to the original intention, and meaning of the biblical text.

Harold Camping Examined

It is now time to examine Harold Camping's teachings directly. As those familiar with Family Radio know, the majority of his teaching is done orally: that is, Camping's teachings are primarily found in his Bible studies and in his answers given on his Open Forum program. But, he has also chosen to put his new teaching in print as well in a booklet entitled, *Has the Era of the Church Age Come to An End?* I have chosen to take the primary documentation from the printed source, and to include after these representative samples of his teaching from his Bible studies. The following chapters include citations of his oral teachings derived from various Family Radio programs as well as a lengthy Open Forum section dealing with this doctrine. Hopefully, by utilizing these varying sources we can give a full-orbed representation of his teaching.

Of course, it bears repeating that no matter how fully we respond to Mr. Camping, his followers will point to some other verse we did not include, and on this basis ignore the rebuttal offered. We have already seen this mindset in operation, unfortunately. Further, there are many times when Camping presents a very elaborate argument that goes on and on, but is based upon a fallacious opening statement. Logically, if one demonstrates the error at the root of the argument, the rest becomes irrelevant. But logic is not the hallmark of Camping's presentations; hence, his followers tend to think that an argument can have merit even when its foundation has been washed away. There is not much that can be done to counter such thinking, other than praying that God will be merciful and allow such folks to see the error of their way.

■ Has the Era of the Church Age Come to an End?

Family Radio compiled a series of articles Camping wrote as he developed his new teaching and placed them in a small booklet entitled, *Has the Era of the Church Age Come to an End?* It contains the main elements of Camping's position, and will allow us to refute his assertions in a point-by-point fashion. Camping begins:

> What is going on? Certainly something strange is happening. On the one hand we see churches every where becoming more and more apostate. Yet on the other hand we see a ministry like Family Radio becoming more and more useful to the Lord in sending the true Gospel into the world.
>
> Virtually everyone of us, as we look at the church we attend, and as we look at the other churches in our city, deplore what we are seeing. The worship service has become increasingly a time of entertainment. The preaching seldom, if ever, warns of the immanence of Judgment Day. Church after church feature signs and wonders. Little or no money is available for mission work because of increasing obligations to pay for newer and finer buildings, and greater and greater pastor's salaries.
>
> Perhaps one of the most shocking experiences of the true believer within these churches is the rejection he will experience if he contends too strongly for greater purity in doctrine.
>
> Indeed any spiritually minded believer must admit something drastic has happened and is happening in even the most conservative of the churches.
>
> How can it be then that a ministry like Family Radio appears to be increasingly blessed as it is able to share the true Gospel with an increasingly large percentage of the world's population.

Mr. Camping does not begin his presentation on solid ground. His personal observations are very limited, of course. Surely we all see apostasy in so-called "churches" across the land, but every person in solid, Bible-centered churches has already learned to differentiate between the wheat and the chaff. One can loudly decry the apostasy that is rampant in many churches without attacking the church

itself. Paul decried the heresy that had infested the churches in Gala-
tia, but it did not follow that *all* churches in *all* places were on that
basis to be denounced as heretical and dead!

Camping often mixes a small measure of truth into his presentation to make it palpable. Are there churches that are focused upon
entertainment rather than the faithful proclamation of the Word?
Of course there are! Are there churches that teach only part of the
gospel message, and not the whole of it? Of course there are! Does
that mean *every* church suffers from these defects? In no way! Do
those who seek to honor God by honoring His truth find themselves
ostracized at times in American evangelicalism? Surely. But does any
of this indicate a complete apostasy, a defection of truth on the part
of the body of Christ *as a whole*? Surely not.

It is amazing, then, to contemplate the attitude portrayed by
Mr. Camping in contrasting the church with his own ministry. Seemingly he wishes us to think that God's blessings rest solely upon
Family Radio and not upon the church. So is Family Radio free of
sin? Is Family Radio perfect? Surely not! So upon what basis does he
identify Family Radio's situation as one of "blessing" while closing
his eyes tightly to the many sound churches that continue faithfully
to honor God in the proclamation of His truth? The irony of all of
this is that much of Family Radio's growth over the years has come
from cooperation with sound local churches, and the funding has
often come from the members of the very churches Camping now
decries!

But do not miss the pregnant phrase, "spiritually minded believers" as it appears in Camping's writing. This is, sadly, a very common phrase in the writings of those who abandon the faith and promote error. Jehovah's Witnesses taught that any "spiritually minded
believer" would be able to observe the events prior to 1914 and see
that Christ had, in fact, returned invisibly in 1874. Of course, their
teachings have changed since then, just as Camping's 1994 prediction failed as well. But in any case, it is always the stance of the person seeking to draw away disciples after himself to make his or her
followers think they are "spiritually minded" while those who
would dare to respond to them are not. This sets up an "us vs. them"
mentality that is very useful in helping to deflect criticism, especially
when that criticism includes the factual refutation of the new teaching being promoted.

■ Prophecies of Church Apostasy

> We do know that there are many prophecies in the Bible
> that indicate that as the history of the world draws to a
> close the congregations and denominations will be increas-
> ingly apostate. For example, Revelation 13 speaks of a time
> when Satan, called the beast that comes out of the sea, will
> rule in the churches through false Gospels. In this chapter
> these churches are called a false prophet that comes out of
> the earth.
>   These churches have become altogether apostate.
>   Fact is verse 7 ominously warns *"And it was given unto
> him [the beast] to make war with the saints and overcome
> them"*. Likewise in 2 Thessalonians 2:1–10 God speaks of
> the man of sin who can only be Satan, taking his seat in the
> temple—that is he will rule in the churches that have be-
> come apostate.

Mr. Camping's use of the Bible, as will be proven repeatedly, is inher-
ently flawed. He will normally begin with a proposition, a statement, and then use a biblical passage to support his statement. This
is the way of the eisegete (the one reading into the text rather than
reading *out* of the text its natural meaning). He sets up a context, an
assertion, and then expects the citation of the biblical passage to
"prove" the point. Here he tells us, prior to providing us with anything other than his own authority, that the Bible prophesies a day
when congregations and denominations will be increasingly apostate. Some eschatological viewpoints would agree with this, some
would not. But in any case, we do not have references in the Bible to
"denominations" to begin with, so Mr. Camping is already expand-
ing upon the biblical witness.

What evidence does Camping offer? He first goes to an apocalyptic section of Scripture, the book of Revelation. History shows us
that almost every person in Camping's position eventually runs to
an a-contextual citation of passages from Revelation to support
their position. Apocalyptic literature in general is easily misused in
this fashion. You can always say, "This represents this, and hence,
my point is proven." This is exactly what Camping does. Without
giving us any background to the passage, any consistent argumenta-

tion to demonstrate the basis of his assertion, he assigns meanings to several of the creatures and characters in Revelation 13 and on this basis "proves" his point. He says the beast is Satan. Camping's entire position must always first answer a simple question when it makes such claims: "Why?" Why should we believe this? Where does the text tell us this? Why isn't the dragon Satan, since that is a much more common term for him? Why should we conclude Satan appears here at all? He may, but the mere announcement of Camping's viewpoint does not provide substantiation thereof. He tells us Satan will "rule" in the churches by "false Gospels." What does this mean? Where does the text say this? Doesn't the text say that *everyone* on earth will worship him, not just apostate churches? These kinds of blanket statements are the sum and substance of Camping's "teaching," and yet they carry no more weight than can be invested in Camping as an individual.

When citing 2 Thessalonians we encounter another commonly used tool of the eisegete: "God speaks of the man of sin who can only be Satan...." Can only be? Who says? Upon what basis are we to accept this claim? There are no other possibilities? Of course there are! And even beyond this, how do we know that what is being discussed in that passage is in any way, shape, or form related to what was in Revelation 13? Does Camping take the time to establish the connection? No, he does not. The connection exists solely because Harold Camping insists it does, nothing more. *Solus Campingus.*

But it should be realized that while we cannot begin to accept this kind of authoritarian, non-textually based eisegesis as having any relevance to the actual message of Scripture, Camping will use such assertions as the basis of his next level of "proof," and then the next, and so on. He will glibly say, "Well, we have already seen how the Bible says this..." and then repeat a previously stated private opinion as if it is now the very Word of God itself. The result is a convoluted structure of utterly unfounded opinions masquerading as biblical exegesis. Such is the lot of the allegorical interpreter.

In Daniel 8:10–14, God speaks of a time when the sanctuary and the host will be trodden under foot for a period of 2300 days, the saints of the most high shall be given into his hand.

While the passage speaks of a period of 2300 days, it nowhere makes the connection that Camping here makes. The ease with which he strings together completely unrelated texts seemingly convinces many listeners that he *must* know what he's talking about since he knows *so many* Bible passages. But stringing Bible passages together, even from memory, does not mean you have fairly, or accurately, dealt with the texts you are citing, and such is the case here as well.

> We all are familiar with the prophecy of Matthew 24:24 which teaches that false Christs and false prophets coming with signs and wonders will arise to deceive the very elect.

Of course, the passage does not say that the false Christs will deceive the elect. This is a simple misrepresentation of the passage. The text actually reads, "so as to mislead, if possible, even the elect." It is not possible to finally deceive the elect, and the citation of this passage, along with the other already cited (and misused) passages is to convey an ever more false impression. But, of course, Mr. Camping has only just begun.

> Indeed these are a sampling of many such prophecies in the Bible. We who love our church because it has been such a comfort to us in the past and even to some degree in the present are not a bit happy to contemplate all of these dire predictions.

Unless, of course, we take into consideration the truths of the Bible regarding the nature, mission, and purpose of the church, and realize that Mr. Camping has not yet cited a single passage that is even remotely relevant to the topic of the church itself!

> They shock us to the core of our being. As we look at the congregation we presently attend we would like to believe that these prophecies must be for another time. Surely the present situation cannot be as bad as these prophecies intimate.

Or, more biblically, these passages are not prophecies about the church at all, and God's promise to continue to build His church in a visible manner continues on unchanged, Mr. Camping's misunderstandings not withstanding.

■ The Eternal Versus Visible Church

At this point Camping goes into a lengthy discussion of the growth of the human population, concluding that,

> Indeed we must realistically admit the churches of today cannot by any means fulfill Christ's command to go into all the world with the Gospel. Fact is, if we honestly evaluate the totality of the mission effort that is based on a true presentation of the whole counsel of God, we must admit the situation is hopeless.

We must admit no such thing, of course. "With men it is impossible, but with God, all things are possible." No reasonable person can possibly accept this kind of glib dismissal of God's ability to use the church to evangelize the world. Are not all the resources that are available to Family Radio available to the church as a whole? Of course, and it must be remembered that for Camping, "the whole counsel of God" means "as Harold Camping interprets it." The fact that there are faithful men and women laboring diligently in the work of spreading the gospel seems to escape Mr. Camping's attention. But they are there, and we show them deep disrespect when we countenance Mr. Camping's foolishness.

> It is true that these external corporate bodies (which include all [sic] of the congregations and denominations that believe that the Bible is the Word of God) are holy organisms established more or less according to Biblical rules. For example in 1 Timothy 3 God has given very careful rules for the selection of elders and deacons. But these churches and denominations have no guarantee of length of time of existence. For example in Revelation 2 and Revelation 3 God speaks of seven churches that were in existence at the time the Bible was being finished. Yet a few hundred years later all of these churches had disappeared. Indeed afterwards for many hundreds of years there was no Christian witness of any kind in the cities wherein these churches had been

located. Thus we can be certain that the church Christ has in view in Matthew 16 is not the corporate external church.

We have already, in a positive fashion, demonstrated the error here presented by Camping, and will note it again in the next chapter. To distinguish as he does between the visible church in particular local congregations and the eternal church is one thing: but the unexpressed assertion Camping is making (and which he could never defend) is that the destructibility of a single local congregation, or even a group of them, does not imply the destructibility of the entirety of all local congregations that make up the visible church of Jesus Christ on earth. Yes, individual congregations can, and do, pass from the scene. But the church is not made up of a *single* congregation, but of the whole aggregate of the elect who have been drawn to Christ. And until the Spirit of God stops calling God's elect to Himself, the church will be alive and well, functioning just as her Lord intended for her to function.

> What church is it then that Jesus had in view when He said "the gates of Hell shall not prevail against It"? The solution is that there is an eternal church which is made up of all those individuals who personally have become saved. They were given eternal life because Jesus as their Savior had paid for each and every one of their sins. Therefore, for evermore they had become safe and secure, Matthew 16 very definitely has this spiritual church in view. It can never come under the wrath of God which is the essence of Hell.

That is true, as far as it goes. However, what Mr. Camping does not seem to realize is that God saves those people *in time and history.* And when God saves His elect, He adds them to the church. The perpetuity of the existence of local congregations of Christ's church is just as certain as the work of the Spirit in applying the redemption God has decreed for His people. To separate the two is unbiblical.

> Therefore, we can know that the corporate external church known as congregations and denominations have no assurance that they are safe from the wrath of God. As a matter

of fact God declared in 1 Peter 4:17 *"judgment must begin at the house of God."*

Since the true believers within a congregation cannot come under God's wrath, this warning was particularly leveled against the corporate or external body.

This is a most confusing and self-contradictory assertion. Is Camping asserting that the congregations that ceased to exist when the Muslims swept across North Africa were under God's wrath? Is he seriously asserting that all the true believers had left these fellowships? Is it not within God's freedom to remove the blessing of a growing, healthy, lively church from a nation without making it a matter of His *wrath* against the church?

Next, his use of 1 Peter 4:17 shows not the first concern for the actual context of the passage. Note Peter's actual words in 4:14–17:

If you are reviled for the name of Christ, you are blessed, because the Spirit of glory and of God rests on you. Make sure that none of you suffers as a murderer, or thief, or evildoer, or a troublesome meddler; but if *anyone suffers* as a Christian, he is not to be ashamed, but is to glorify God in this name. For *it is* time for judgment to begin with the household of God; and if *it begins* with us first, what *will be* the outcome for those who do not obey the gospel of God?

One immediately notices the complete misuse of the passage by Camping: if he has just finished saying that the wrath of God comes only upon external congregations, how can he then use a passage that says *in the very next phrase*, "and if it begins with us first, what will be the outcome for those who do not obey the gospel of God?" Can he not see that this defines, without question, that the "household of God" is made up of those who *have* obeyed the gospel of God? And can he not see that the preceding verses define this judgment not in the form of wrath against "high places" or sin or anything else, but in the form of discipline and sanctification? To take this one phrase, wrench it from its context, and use it as Camping does (repeatedly) is inexcusable.

> But a serious question must be raised. It is true that God brought the seven churches spoken of in the book of Revelation into judgment by removing them. But isn't it also true that throughout the New Testament era churches or denominations do disappear. But aren't they replaced by other churches and denominations that are more faithful? Worldwide hasn't there always been in existence a core group of faithful churches? For example, even today are there not a sprinkling of faithful churches that are at least as true to the Word of God as many churches were several hundred years ago?
>
> This is true! But there is a larger plan of God that must be looked at.

This statement is actually quite saddening, as it demonstrates that Mr. Camping is not ignorant of the truth regarding this topic. He well knows it, but buries it under his personal agenda: that of promoting his own teaching at the expense of biblical truth.

> This plan shows that a time will come when God will no longer use the churches and congregations to bring the Gospel to the world. They instead will come under the wrath of God.

Such is Mr. Camping's scheme, but so far, we have not seen the first serious attempt to establish a basis for this assertion. But dig as we may into his teachings, we will never find the biblical foundation, for there is none.

> To see this plan we must carefully examine Old Testament Israel. They, without any question, typify the New Testament church which the Bible speaks of as the Israel of God. (Gal. 6:16)

Old Testament Israel "without any question" typifies the New Testament church, so that Mr. Camping is given a basis for ransacking the Old Testament to find "types" to use to teach the destruction of the church? Such is a tacit admission that no meaningful exegesis of the passages in Scripture that directly address the nature and purpose of the church will be found to be supportive of Camping's teachings. He is forced to create inconsistent, arbitrary "pictures" from whatever passages catch his eye to create the "biblical basis" of his attack upon the church.

At this point Camping transitions into a lengthy discussion of Old Testament passages, including the concept of the "high places" in Israel. These were places of idolatrous worship, the "groves" or "Asheriim" that were common to Canaanite religion. Instead of focusing upon the true meaning of the high places (the lack of devotion to the worship of the one true God) Camping emphasizes that these high places represented the rebellious exaltation of man's own mind (so as to more closely parallel them with what he identifies as "high places" in modern churches). He then attempts to bring these parallels into focus in our own day by saying,

> With this background in view we must ask the logical question -What (*sic*) does the destruction of ancient Israel in 709 B.C. and 587 B.C. have to do with us today. The answer must come to us loud and clear. What God did to ancient Israel has everything to do with this matter. In Hebrews 13:8 the Bible declares *"Jesus Christ the same yesterday and today and tomorrow."* Jesus is Jehovah God of the Old Testament. As we view His treatment of ancient Israel we can know how He deals with the New Testament Israel, the churches and congregations that exist all over the world.

Yes, Jesus Christ is the same yesterday, today, and forever, but that obviously does not have the slightest to do with the current topic of discussion! Jesus Christ is the same yesterday and today and tomorrow, but that does not mean that we have a Levitical priesthood, that we sacrifice animals, that we do not wear mixed-material clothing, that we should be looking for the opening of the Red Sea, or should build temples that keep out Gentiles. Just because Jesus does not change does not mean God deals with the church, the body of Christ, the way he did with Israel. When was Israel's "Pentecost," for example? Who were the spirit-filled elders and deacons? Where is the supernatural oneness the Spirit gives Christians in someone like Ahab, or Jezebel? Israel was a mixed company, a rebellious and stiff-necked people in general, with a small remnant that was faithful to God. Does Mr. Camping teach the church is likewise made up only of a remnant? Has he not encountered Hebrews 8:6–13? Even if we were to grant Camping the idea of direct parallelism to the Old Testament, upon what basis should we conclude he is correctly interpreting the right parallels and types? We have yet to see him accurately utilize the text of Scripture in the context of his new teaching, so why should we have confidence in him at all?

■ 2 Corinthians 10:4–6

But is it true, that our churches are free of high places? The Bible shows us that the churches of today are not at all free of the high places. The Bible defines the nature of the New Testament high places in 2 Corinthians 10:4–6. There we read: *for the weapons of our warfare are not carnal, but mighty through God to the pulling down of strongholds: casting down imaginations and every high thing that exalteth itself against the knowledge of God, and bringing into captivity every thought to the obedience of Christ and having in a readiness to revenge all disobedience when your obedience is fulfilled.*

Immediately we note that "high thing" and "high places" are not synonymous terms, so Camping's claim is suspect from the start. But it is his complete misrepresentation of the text that we need to expose at this point. A little later in his presentation Camping makes application of this text in these words:

Ominously, the passage in 2 Corinthians 10:4–6 which speaks of the New Testament high places also warns of a time when God will destroy the high places. Remember God said *"for the weapons of our warfare are not carnal but mighty through God...having in a readiness to revenge all disobedience when your obedience is fulfilled."* In this very revealing passage God is declaring that punishment will come when the obedience of the churches will have been fulfilled. That is, their work of sending the Gospel into the world has been finished.

First, no effort has been made to explain how this passage refers to "high places." Does the mere repetition of the word "high" somehow indicate identity? So is the "most high God" likewise a phrase referring to idolatry? Of course not. So just because the word "high" appears means nothing. The only meaningful way Mr. Camping could draw a parallel would be to establish it by context, something he does not do.

The context of the passage likewise demonstrates the error of his use of it. Paul is writing to the Corinthian church. There are those in the fellowship who oppose his authority and question his teaching (a fact found in the immediate context, 2 Corinthians 10:8–11). The strength of his first letter, and the authority he exercised therein, caused some to stumble. Note the beginning words of this chapter:

> Now I, Paul, myself urge you by the meekness and gentleness of Christ—I who am meek when face to face with you, but bold toward you when absent! I ask that when I am present I *need* not be bold with the confidence with which I propose to be courageous against some, who regard us as if we walked according to the flesh. (2 Corinthians 10:1–2)

There were those who were saying Paul and his companions were fleshly, not truly "spiritual" (like "they" were). This is the context in which Paul is speaking. It is directly relevant to the congregation at Corinth. He is warning that he as an apostle of Christ does not engage in conflict on a merely human level, but a spiritual level. The weapons of this warfare are not material weapons, such as swords or knives, but are divine in origin, and hence are able to destroy "fortresses." These fortresses are not physical buildings, of course, but "speculations and every lofty thing raised up against the knowledge of God." To what is Paul referring? Camping's "high places," or the arguments and rebellious attitudes of those in Corinth who were opposing his ministry in the church? The answer is plain. The apostles, Paul says, are taking every thought captive unto the obedience of Christ. While this phrase is often used in a very general fashion (with greater or lesser levels of merit), in its original context Paul is speaking of the specific situation in the church at Corinth. He is referring to those who are opposing him, and he is saying in plain words that their thoughts are opposed to Christ. He leaves no neutral ground.

This then provides the context of Paul's statement, "and we are ready to punish all disobedience, whenever your obedience is complete." Camping makes the amazing assertion that "In this very revealing passage God is declaring that punishment will come when the obedience of the churches will have been fulfilled. That is, their work of sending the Gospel into the world has been finished." Of course, such is another glowing example of eisegesis. First, Paul says that "*we* are ready," that is, Paul and his companions. Obviously, he was referring to the Corinthian church. How Camping can jump from this to some general statement about the entirety of the visible church two thousand years later is impossible to say. Paul is saying that he and his companions will, upon the restoration of the church at Corinth to obedience to apostolic authority, punish every act of disobedience against that authority. To read into these words some future prophecy about the end of the church age is simply ridiculous on its face. Camping's, "That is, their work of sending the Gospel into the world has been finished," has no basis in the text, and Camping does not even attempt to provide a logical connection for his complete misreading of the words of Scripture.

It may seem repetitive, but it needs to be pointed out yet once again, that while we have seen Camping's arguments falter time and again, he builds his entire system upon these foundational arguments. Logically, then, the entire position crumbles to the ground when the test of consistency and truth is applied to it. But many of Camping's followers prefer not to see it in this way, but instead retreat to another portion of the structure, never seeing how the whole thing collapses under its own weight.

■ Attack Upon Confessions

During the Old Testament days it took serious thought as to how to properly design and build a high place in order to make the overall worship scene more complete.[1] In the New Testament[2] serious men have carefully thought about teachings they felt were pleasing to God. They reasoned together in solemn meetings such as church councils, consistories and synods. After prayerful consideration they adopted doctrines which were not always true to the Bible. Some of the erroneous conclusions were even written into and became a part of very prestigious confessions. This was so even though they had arrived at conclusions that were not taught in the Bible. Such conclusions that there can be divorce for fornication, baptismal regeneration, our faith is an instrument that God uses to bring us to salvation, a future millennium, women can pastor a church, universal atonement, our acceptance of Christ as a requirement for salvation, are typical of many doctrines solemnly adopted by churches. But these are high places, in that they have come from the exalted minds of men instead of coming from God.

We have already examined this list of alleged "high places" when we presented the general outline of Camping's teaching, and noted at that time a mixture of truth and error therein. In any situation when we disagree with the conclusions of those who, at the very least, believe the Bible to be the inspired Word of God, Jesus to be the incarnate Son of God who died on Calvary and rose again the third day, and who confess a willingness to submit entirely to the Scriptures and the Scriptures alone (which would describe all of those churches Camping is referring to in the above quoted section), we owe a simple debt of honor and respect to provide a sound basis for our disagreement. We should honestly and accurately represent the position of those with whom we disagree, and our own presentation should partake of a conscious recognition of our own failings and imperfections. We have tried to model this by beginning our examination of Harold Camping's teaching with both a fair and accurate representation of his own position as well as a biblically-based, consistent presentation of the doctrine of the church (against which Camping inveighs constantly). But it is just this equity and fairness in debate that Mr. Camping refuses to offer to the entirety of the church his ministry once professed to assist! He lists as "high places" that bring God's judgment upon the church a list of beliefs that, at the very least, contains a few items that are subject to dispute by men of God who are far more knowledgeable in the Scriptures than Harold Camping. So how can he so boldly proclaim this list without acknowledging this? It is difficult to say.

Is it true that some churches, especially Reformed churches, can enshrine in their confessions an authority that is inconsistent even with their own self-professed belief in the ultimacy of Scripture? Of course it is. Should every church be consistent with its own principles and be willing to examine its confession of faith in the light of Scripture? Yes. But should all churches be ready to abandon their confessions of faith (which are merely to function as summaries of biblical truth) simply because a single individual radio preacher with a bad prophetic track record engages in a lengthy spate of allegorical interpretation and comes to conclusions no scholar or theologian before him has ever seen? Or should such a singular voice be rejected, not because it is alone, but because it is obviously not speaking with the voice of Scripture?

■ Revelation 11 and the Two Witnesses

This coincides with the warning of Revelation 11 that the time will come when the work of the church to bring the Gospel, as typified by the two witnesses, is finished. The two witnesses will be killed. Rev 11:7 declares *"and when they shall have finished their testimony the beast that ascended out of the bottomless pit shall make war against them and shall overcome them and shall kill them."*

We have already seen the necessity of placing Mr. Camping's citations in their original contexts. This is especially true when looking at his use of passages from the book of Revelation. Are the two witnesses a typology of the church as a whole? Let's read the passage, Revelation 11:3–12, and consider this:

> "And I will grant *authority* to my two witnesses, and they will prophesy for twelve hundred and sixty days, clothed in sackcloth." These are the two olive trees and the two lampstands that stand before the Lord of the earth. And if anyone wants to harm them, fire flows out of their mouth and devours their enemies; so if anyone wants to harm them, he must be killed in this way. These have the power to shut up the sky, so that rain will not fall during the days of their prophesying; and they have power over the waters to turn them into blood, and to strike the earth with every plague, as often as they desire. When they have finished their testi-

mony, the beast that comes up out of the abyss will make war with them, and overcome them and kill them. And their dead bodies *will lie* in the street of the great city which mystically is called Sodom and Egypt, where also their Lord was crucified. Those from the peoples and tribes and tongues and nations *will* look at their dead bodies for three and a half days, and will not permit their dead bodies to be laid in a tomb. And those who dwell on the earth *will* rejoice over them and celebrate; and they will send gifts to one another, because these two prophets tormented those who dwell on the earth. But after the three and a half days, the breath of life from God came into them, and they stood on their feet; and great fear fell upon those who were watching them. And they heard a loud voice from heaven saying to them, "Come up here." Then they went up into heaven in the cloud, and their enemies watched them.

One is immediately struck by the fact that the basic reading of the text does not in any way suggest these two witnesses are a picture of the church. They testify for a limited amount of time in sackcloth. They are called olive trees and lampstands (Camping only connects with one of the descriptions, but what does the other mean?). They devour their enemies with fire. Like Moses and Elijah, they have power to shut up the sky, or turn water to blood: miraculous powers Camping would never attribute to the church in the New Testament age. They are killed by the beast, to be certain, but ironically, they are killed in Jerusalem. I say ironically because elsewhere Camping inconsistently teaches that Jerusalem represents the church, at least when we are told to flee from it. How can the two witnesses be killed in Jerusalem, when they represent the church and Jerusalem also represents the church? In any case, the two witnesses bodies are left unburied, and they are looked upon by the whole world, resulting in a great celebration, involving the exchanging of gifts. However, after three and a half days, they come back to life, and are then summoned to heaven.

If one only seeks to find "pictures" to use to promote a particular view, and consistency is an expendable notion, you can parallel a few items to the church. But if you seek any consistency whatsoever, it is obviously a lost cause to find a parallel to the two witnesses to the church in each detail given (and is it not Camping who always says that each detail is important?). How does the church, for example, shoot fire from its mouth? Is this the gospel? And the resurrection of the two witnesses on earth: does this mean the church will be resurrected as well *on earth*? Attempting to make a consistent presentation out of this kind of whimsical, capricious grasping at passages and creation of "pictures" of the church under judgment is simply impossible.

> Earlier in Revelation 11 God had explained in verse 4 that the two witnesses are the two olive trees and the two candlesticks standing before the God of the earth. Remember in Revelation 1:20 and Revelation 2:1 God had indicated that each candlestick represents a church. Therefore, when the two witnesses are killed because their work had been finished it meant that the church is dead-the candlestick no longer can give light. That is, God is no longer using the church to bring the Gospel.

The text speaks of "their testimony," not of the work of the church. If Mr. Camping were consistent, he'd have to admit that the candlesticks in Revelation 1 and 2 are individual local congregations, not the entirety of all congregations. So, if he insists on ignoring the olive-tree description and making any application there (is that not Israel, or maybe some kind of messianic reference? Who is to say?), why not at least strive for some level of uniformity and say these two witnesses represent *two congregations* who, upon completing their testimony in a hostile world, are destroyed, only to come back to life as testimony of God's grace and power? At least such an interpretation would not be completely arbitrary. But instead, the over-riding thrust for Camping is the attempted substantiation of that final assertion: God is no longer using the church to preach the gospel. And if the church is not being used to spread the gospel, who is? Well, Family Radio, of course.

> Therefore we see clearly that God has predetermined a time during the New Testament era when punishment would come against high things and exalted reasonings of men. This punishment would take place when the obedience of

the churches had been fulfilled. We have already seen that the obedience was fulfilled when the work of the two witnesses had been finished.

We once again see the mechanics of Camping's false teachings clearly exposed: "We see clearly" when there is nothing to be seen; "the obedience of the churches" has already been shown to be a misinterpretation (and misrepresentation, as Paul does not use the plural "churches"); and no one has "seen" that the words of Paul to the Corinthians about a particular situation in history has the slightest thing to do with the two witnesses in Revelation 11. Eisegesis, coupled with unfounded assertions, mixed with fanciful allegories: this is the substance of Harold Camping's "Bible teaching."

> This identifies with the warning of 1 Peter 4:17, "For the time has come that judgment must begin at the house of God." The event of this judgment on the churches is a terrible blow to them. In a way it is as traumatic and awful as the destruction of ancient Judah by the Babylonians in 587 B.C. Therefore, God speaks of this event as a time of great tribulation. In Matthew 24:21 the Bible declares there will be great tribulation such as this world has never known or ever shall know.

As the misinterpretations and unfounded claims pile upon one another, the clear outlines of the entire system come into view. The same passages that have been used in the past (and seen to be misused) surface over and over again whenever there is a felt need to provide some kind of "glue" to hold together the wildly disconnected streams of "evidence" Camping tries to put together. It seems only the person who is repeatedly exposed to this kind of teaching, and willingly seeks to embrace it, can be convinced by this kind of presentation. Indeed, it has been the observation of many elders in the church that those who find such assertions compelling are often (not always) those who either seek out "new" things, new movements, etc., or those who are seeking a way out from under the God-ordained authority of the church. In other words, you have to *want to* believe these tortured lines of reasoning to end up doing so.

■ Signs and Wonders?

One of the more intriguing aspects of Camping's teachings has to do with his unusual assertions regarding "signs and wonders." Now surely, there is much to be said in very valid criticism of what is done under the name of "signs and wonders" in our day. But Mr. Camping's comments even on this subject where, it would seem, it would be so easy to provide clear, compelling, and contextually accurate criticisms of the excesses and errors of the signs and wonders movement, give evidence of his inability or unwillingness to engage in meaningful exegetical study. Instead of focusing upon the real issues that need to be addressed, Mr. Camping makes the existence of the phenomena of falling backward on the ground evidence that we are indeed in the time of the tribulation! If it were not for the seriousness of the issue, the following attempts at stringing together biblical texts would simply be humorous.

> Never before in all of church history has there been such an interest in signs and wonders, miracles, such as we see to-day. All over the world there is an intense interest in this kind of activity. This evidence alone assures us that we are living in the period of the great tribulation.

One wonders, in passing, how Mr. Camping knows this. There have, in fact, been intense periods of interest in just such things (Montanism being an example from the past). Yes, the availability of the very forms of communication Camping identifies as God's means of spreading the gospel through Family Radio (television, radio, the Internet) has allowed this kind of teaching to spread far and wide in a way it never could before.

> A second evidence is the world wide evidence of people falling backward. The churches that practice this miracle call it "being slain in the Spirit."
> This miracle was foretold in Revelation 13. The whole chapter is describing the great tribulation period. In verse 13 we read:
> *"And he doeth great wonders, so that he maketh fire come down from heaven on the earth in the sight of men."*
> Satan, of course, cannot literally call down fire from

heaven. This is proven by the contest between the 450 prophets of Baal, who were Satans (*sic*) emissaries, and Elijah. But God gave Satan a demonstration that showed that causing someone to fall backward was equivalent to calling down fire from heaven.

In case the reader is losing track of where Mr. Camping is going, in essence, he is about to "prove" that Revelation 13 predicts the "slain in the Spirit" phenomena, but does so under the idea of calling fire down from heaven. Of course, already, we might point out that maybe it is Camping who has missed the point of both Revelation 13 *and* the contest between the priests of Baal and Elijah? Could it be that the beast mentioned in Revelation 13 isn't Satan? And could it be that God, being sovereign over all things, withheld the forces of evil from performing a great miracle in the days of Elijah? One might suppose. But he goes on.

In 2 Kings 1 we read about the wicked king of Israel who sent a captain with 50 men with a command to Elijah that he was to come to the king. Elijah caused fire to come down and destroy these men. Likewise in Revelation 20 we read about the nations from the four quarters of the earth surrounding the camp of the saints, and fire from heaven came down and destroyed them.

There is another incident recorded in the Bible when Satan wished to conquer the kingdom of God. That occurred when Jesus came out of the Garden of Gethsemene. There stood the emissaries of Satan, the temple servants, together with Judas who was in filled by Satan and they desired to bind Jesus and have Him crucified. At that moment Jesus following the example of Elijah or of God in Revelation 20:10 should have called for fire to come down and destroy these wicked men.

But Jesus had to be bound and taken to be crucified. This was an integral part of the atonement. However, to show that He had the power to call down fire from heaven and destroy them, when He answered them Jesus caused all of these wicked men to fall backward to the ground.

Satan, therefore, was an eyewitness to the fact that

causing people to fall backward to the ground is equivalent
to calling down fire from heaven.

It is difficult to find the words to respond to such "interpretations,"
but we have included this section as another glowing example of the
kind of "interpretation" that Camping presents as being so basic
and clear that everyone should be able to see it. And yet, as hopefully
all our readers can see, there is not the first bit of rational connection
between the passages Camping cites. Calling down fire from heaven
is not the same as falling backward. Camping simply never contem-
plates the possibility that once he has "decided" a thing (such as
"Satan cannot bring fire down from heaven") then it is simply impossible that he may have missed something along the way. This
kind of mindset leads many to a state of unteachability: once they
decide an issue, even if it is of minor importance, they make it a matter of utter importance and hold to it with dogged tenacity. God
built a safeguard into His wise ordering of the church that is meant
to curb this kind of error: the plurality of elders. But Mr. Camping is
not under the authority of elders, let alone fellow elders, and hence
he roams the eisegetical range with impunity, nibbling on this topic
or that before moving on to the next. Such is the danger of rejecting
God's wise provision: it leads to a deceptive certainty rather than a
biblical one. That kind of certainty comes out in Camping's words,
such as these:

> We can be certain that the 144,000 are the complete fullness
> of all those who would became saved by the activity of the
> churches during the New Testament era. But as we learned
> from Revelation 11 and 2 Corinthians 10 there would come
> a time when the work of the churches was finished.

Camping offers the empty shell of "certainty" to his followers: empty, for it in reality has no connection to the Word of God, which
alone can give true certainty and confidence. He gives an unfounded, arbitrary interpretation of a number in Revelation (the
144,000), calls it a certainty, and then repeats the already refuted
assertions about the end of the church age from Revelation 11 and 2
Corinthians 10. New errors, joined with old errors, growing into
ever-greater error.

Because we witness this phenomena by a ministry such as Family Radio which in no sense is under the authority of the church and which tries to be as faithful to the Bible as possible, we can know that we are in that time of the great tribulation. The next event will be the return of Christ and the end of the world.

And so Mr. Camping said prior to 1994 as well, and he was wrong then, too. One truly wonders about the head of a ministry that views his own work as a "phenomena" that somehow heralds the end of the world. But then again, Mr. Camping has been willing to stand alone and proclaim the death and destruction of Christ's church while claiming the blessing of God upon his own work, so we should not be overly surprised.

■ Flee the Churches!

When Mr. Camping first began to introduce his anti-church teachings on his radio programs, and especially on the Open Forum, he was hesitant to come directly out and tell people to leave their churches. But it did not take long for that to change. He is now openly telling believers to flee their churches. Given that we have already seen that Camping has no biblical basis for this teaching, he is guilty of exhorting believers to abandon the God-given means of protection and sanctification, to rebel against the leaders He has provided in His grace (Hebrews 13:17), and to wander off into the no-mans land of "fellowship" that has no form, no order, and no direction. Camping raises the issue in these words:

> And that brings us to a very real but very troublesome question. If we can still find or are still a part of a church that is reasonably true to the Bible, should we remain there? Does the Bible give us clear instruction concerning this very important question? Fact is, what are we to do if we could find a church where it appears that each and every doctrine they hold and teach is faithful to the Word of God?

We pause only long enough to note that for Camping, this question is *only* for those who, somehow, find themselves in a church that believes *exactly* like Harold Camping. Even the smallest disagreement with him, especially on those matters that make up his list of "high places," automatically places one outside even this very limited question.

To answer this question we must re-examine God's commands to ancient Israel when Babylon had destroyed Jerusalem.

One simply asks, "Why?" But by now the answer to that is known: "Because Mr. Camping says so." If Mr. Camping says the commands to Jews in one particular situation regarding God's judgment upon Jerusalem at the beginning of the sixth century B.C. are relevant, then it is—period. What the New Testament says about the church, its purposes and perpetuity, is really not relevant. The follower of Harold Camping is left with only one guide: Harold Camping. *Solus Campingus.*

Significantly God declares in Luke 21:20–24:

"And when ye shall see Jerusalem compassed with armies, then know that the desolation thereof is nigh. Then let them which are in Judea flee to the mountains; and let them which are in the midst of it depart out; and let not them that are in the countries enter thereinto. For these be the days of vengeance, that all things which are written may be fulfilled."

Please notice that God is not saying that when we *experience* Jerusalem is surrounded by armies. Rather it is saying that when we *see* Jerusalem surrounded by armies. Jerusalem or Judea represent all of the New Testament churches and denominations. When we see, as we do see, Satan's massive attack on churches all over the world we are to depart out.

As we noted above, in his drive to create a basis for his teaching, Camping turns Jerusalem both into the place where the two witnesses (representing the church, we are told) died *and* into a picture of the church as well! In any case, we are told with the typical Camping confidence that "Jerusalem or Judea represent all of the New Testament churches and denominations." Oh? Why? Who says? Upon what logical or rational basis is this assertion made? Where does the Bible make this statement? We are not told. *Solus Campingus*. But on the basis of this capricious identification Camping tells us that we are to "depart out" when we "see" the massive attack Camping posits. Though he did not make this comment in the written portion of his work, when he addressed this same passage in his radio program,[3] he informed his listeners that the reason we should believe that Jerusalem is a picture of the church is because it simply could not refer to either the "Jerusalem above" nor to the historical or present day Jerusalem. Note his words,

> Now Jesus says it very plainly in Luke 21, "When you see Jerusalem surrounded by armies...." And the only Jerusalem we can talk about are the corporate body.... It's not talking about the Jerusalem above, the true believers, because we can't escape that Jerusalem, we are eternally there, we are eternal citizens of the spiritual, heavenly Jerusalem. And it's not talking about the literal Jerusalem over there alongside the Mediterranean Sea, because that has nothing to do with the whole Christian, the whole Bible emphasis of our day, so what other Jerusalem is there? It's the corporate body, the external body of churches and congregations that God is talking about. And when you see Jerusalem surrounded by armies, let those who are in Judea flee to the mountains, and that's a figure of speech, flee to Christ. And then it says, "And those that are within her, depart out." Now that's a plain command that God is giving.

So the reason Jesus' reference to "Jerusalem" must be a picture of the congregations and churches is that it can't refer to the historical Jerusalem. And why not? Because that would not have anything to do "with the whole...Bible emphasis of our day"! So, the ancient text is to be interpreted not in light of what the original authors would have intended or understood, but as what is relevant to us in our day, nearly two thousand years removed temporally, and thousands of miles removed geographically! The fact that we can make application of such a warning in many meaningful ways without changing the meaning of the original text escapes Mr. Camping.

This is language that identifies with the great tribulation. In this language God is commanding the same thing He commanded Jerusalem in Jeremiah 29. Get out of Jerusalem (the church).

No longer are you to be under the spiritual rulership of the church.

This command is given because God is finished with the era of churches being used of God to evangelize.

Hence the conclusion of his teaching: based upon clearly inaccurate and unfounded assumptions Camping exhorts his listeners to leave the God-ordained place of blessing, fellowship and protection, and encourages rank rebellion and disobedience by promising his followers that they are no longer to be under the "spiritual rulership of the church." The words of the Lord Jesus come to mind when one hears Camping's teaching, "but whoever causes one of these little ones who believe in Me to stumble, it would be better for him to have a heavy millstone hung around his neck, and to be drowned in the depth of the sea" (Matthew 18:6). God takes His truth very seriously. Camping expands upon his call to ecclesiastical sedition and rebellion:

The message should be clear. We must remove ourself (*sic*) from the church.

In the context of "Remember Lot's wife God also declares in Luke 17:31:

"In that day, he which shall be upon the housetop, and his stuff in the house, let him not come down to take it away: and he that is in the field let him likewise not return back."

The housetop is identified with bringing the Gospel. In Luke 12:3 we read:

"Therefore, whatsoever ye have spoken in darkness shall be heard in the light and that which ye have spoken in the earn closets shall be proclaimed upon the housetops."

The house identifies with the church. But as judgment comes on the church the true believer is to stay outside the church bringing the Gospel to the world.

One is again left speechless at the willy-nilly interpretation of Camping. The two passages are from completely different contexts, but this means nothing to Camping's allegorical interpretation, which ignores all contexts anyway. The first is about fleeing when the destruction of Jerusalem approaches. The second is about the fact that nothing hidden will not be made known in God's judgment. To proclaim something from the housetop was to make sure it was known to all around, nothing more. Luke makes no connection between "house" and "housetop," and there is no logical or rational reason to do so. But Camping needs nothing from the text to make such connections: the mere repetition of the word is sufficient. Throw in another example of *Solus Campingus* ("the house identifies with the church") and you have another a-contextual assertion based solely on Camping's authority that we are to flee the church.

> Because the church era has come to an end the churches have become dead as the church of Sardis long ago became dead. (Rev 3:1). The churches of today have had their candle stick removed even as the church of Ephesus of Rev. 2 was warned that God would remove their candlestick if they did not return to their first love. The church has ceased to be an institution or divine organism to serve God as His appointed representative on earth.

One might well speculate as to why Camping would have such a deep desire (despite his professed abhorrence of this teaching) to convince others of these words. Surely, as we have seen, it is not the exegesis of the text of Scripture that leads him here. He would have to be completely self-deceived to believe his own ruminations, and, of course, such is possible. But one must also remember the words of the apostle Paul when he spoke of those who would arise from *within* the ranks of the eldership (Acts 20:28–32). He said these men speak perverse things (and surely, calling people to flee the church amounts to true theological perversity) so that they might "draw away the disciples after them." This seems the best explanation for this kind of activity on Camping's part: the drawing away of disciples after him.

■ **Important Excursus: The Holy Spirit Is Not Active**

One of the most vociferously unbiblical and, if we may be so bold, blasphemous elements of the teaching Harold Camping has developed on the basis of his allegorical interpretations is his repeated assertion that the Holy Spirit of God is no longer active in drawing His elect unto Christ within the sphere of the visible, corporate church. That is, put in plain words, the Spirit of God no longer saves His people inside any formal body of believers (i.e., which is organized upon biblical lines with elders and deacons). Never have Christians put such a limitation upon the almighty Spirit of God. While many have said the Spirit does not save outside of the use of the true gospel, never has anyone seriously suggested that the Spirit of God could be limited, so that if a person were to be attending worship in the very place described in the Scriptures as the abode of the people of God, such a person would be in a place where the Spirit *would not* apply the work of Christ and bring them to salvation. Moreover, given the incredibly poor, self-refuting, inconsistent and, at times, incoherent arguments presented by Camping as the basis of this teaching, it is truly amazing that anyone could possibly accept this incredible conclusion: The Holy Spirit, barred from the very body that is described as His own dwelling place (Ephesians 2:22), is unable, or unwilling, to bring about the miracle of regeneration and the salvation of His people within the church. Camping continually emphasizes that it is "outside" the church, as we will note a little later (based upon a misinterpretation of John 21:6 and other passages), that the work of evangelization and salvation is taking place. Note his words:

> as the gospel is presented today, if the Holy Spirit is not operating there's no one becoming saved.

> During the church, over 1900 years, God did apply the Word of God to the hearts of people, so that even churches that had very bad doctrine were still being used of the Lord to evangelize in the world in wonderful ways. But if the Holy Spirit is not operating, then you could have the most ideal preacher you could name and nobody is becoming saved. Do you want to be there?

And why did He give that command? For the security of the true believers. Because who wants to be in a church that is under the judgment of God? Who wants to be there if the Holy Spirit is not working? Who wants to be there if it is Satan now who has taken his seat in the temple as we read in 2 Thessalonians 2? These are ugly things, these are traumatic things, these are terrible things that I'm talking about, and yet I'm quoting from the Bible. These are not ideas that come out of my mind, I'm quoting from the Bible. This is what God has written about.

The mixture of the very small amount of truth with a great amount of error can be seen in the final quoted paragraph. Surely, *if* one were a part of an apostate church, one should flee, simply out of honor of the truth. But, one would flee *to* the true church, not out into the wilderness of spiritual chaos. The one who honors God's truth will not rebel against the very embodiment of that truth in the Scriptures, which so plainly teach us about the purposes and life of the church.

Camping says these are ugly, traumatic, terrible things that he is talking about, and he is correct. They are. But what makes them so much more ugly and terrible is that they are *untrue,* and transparently so. It would be bad enough if it were simply Mr. Camping who was deceived. It would be sad to see someone who had lived his life in the church wandering off into the wilderness of error. But when he leads others into the same darkness, using the stored credibility of past generations of pastors and teachers who have graced the airwaves of Family Radio as his capital, we have a true tragedy on our hands.

■ Back to the "Command" to Flee

Camping is so firmly convinced of his own "insights" (and seems utterly unconcerned about the fact that he alone has these insights) that he has the audacity to indict *every* elder, *every* deacon, *every* congregation that would dare to believe something other than what he, Harold Camping, concludes is "faithful." The Holy Spirit, seemingly, now reveals His mind through Harold Camping, not through all those who are indwelt by the Spirit and who together come to the same conclusions regarding biblical teachings. Note his words:

It is no wonder that it is almost impossible to find a church today that will modify its Confessions to make them more faithful to the Bible. Remember the Bible says that it is God who works in us to will and to do of His good pleasure. Therefore, if a church no longer has a candlestick it means God is not working in that church. The elders and deacons are being guided by their own minds rather than by the Holy Spirit.

The irony is that Camping repeatedly uses the phrase "by their own minds" when his method of "interpretation" limits him to exactly that: his own mind! He cannot truthfully claim the Bible as his support since his entire methodology mutes the voice of Scripture and replaces it with the imaginations of the heart of the allegorical interpreter. So the one who brings forth the imaginations of his own mind dressed in a-contextual quotes from the Bible arraigns the entirety of those who seek to follow *Sola Scriptura* and utters his judgment: I'm right, they are all wrong. And even more amazing is the fact that some nod in agreement and fall in line behind him.

In the never-ending attempt to find "pictures" of the church so that he can attack it and proclaim its demise, Camping now goes beyond the two witnesses in Revelation, and beyond Jerusalem and Judea, to the very temple buildings themselves (One must truly ask: Is there *anything* that is not liable to be a "picture" of the church?):

> These temple buildings represent the churches and congregations God would build throughout the New Testament time. Those who come into this spiritual temple are gold, silver and precious stones, and wood, hay, stubble (I Cor. 3:12). That is they are both true believers and those who appear to be true believers and actually are not. Thus each congregation is an integral part of that great temple.
>
> But Jesus declares that there will be a time when there will not be left one stone upon another. That is, the temple will be totally destroyed. It will no longer exist.

Using this new "picture" of the church (no foundation for the identification is given, unless the a-contextual citation of a completely different context, that of the judgment of Christian leaders noted by

Paul in 1 Corinthians three, is supposed to function as one) Camping then tells us that even if a congregation were to follow *his* teachings completely, "removing" the "high places," they still could not remain a true church:

> But suppose a congregation believes that it can remove all of the high places. It will endeavor to be as faithful to the Bible as possible.
> It then is insisting that it is still a tiny part of the temple that still exists.

That is, given his understanding that Jesus' words about the stones of the temple (fulfilled, obviously, in A.D. 70) representing the churches, God will destroy *all* the churches, even if they were to "repent" and adopt Harold Camping's theology, lock, stock and barrel. There simply is no more church age, no matter what actions a local congregation may take.

■ Leave the Church, But Fellowship Anyway

> But there is a command that God gives to the post-church believer. It is found in Hebrews 10:25 where God commands:
> *"not forsaking the assembling of ourselves together, as the manner of some is; but exhorting one another: and so much the more, as ye see the day approaching."*
> Significantly the Greek word translated 'assembling' in this verse is only found in one other place and that is in 2 Thess 2:1 where it is the word "gathering together." But this gathering together consists only of true believers because it is a "gathering together unto Him" as Christ comes on the last day. Thus, it is a word that identifies only with true believers. As the end of the world approaches few true believers are found inside the churches because the era of the church as an institution used of God has come to and end.

One of the great tragedies awaiting those who fall into the trap set by Camping's teachings is the experience of the "post-church fellowship." This disorganized body of Camping's followers is doomed to utter failure. Why? Well, it has no divine mandate to exist; it is based upon falsehood; it has no organization, and its only direction is derived from a radio preacher in California, to be blunt about it. Hebrews 10:25 is about fellowship *in the church*, not in some "post-church" amorphous body.

Camping is struggling to come up with "direction" to give to his followers regarding these "fellowships." How do you handle marriage? Burials? What about discipline? The God-ordained means of handling these things have been summarily dismissed by Camping's blanket destruction of the visible church, so what now? No one really knows. Till then he basically draws from the church those things that he himself finds "comfortable." For example,

> True, the Sunday Sabbath is still God's Holy day. It is a day that continues as a day for spiritual activity. But this day no longer focuses on the church as an external institution. Rather it focuses on the eternal body of believers which is also called the eternal church. It is the church over which the gates of Hell cannot prevail (Matt. 16:18).

In "The Debate that Almost Was" we deal with Camping's teaching that the ordinances (the Lord's Supper and Baptism) have been done away with as well. For now, we simply note that Camping does view himself to be in the position to give nigh unto pontifical-style direction to these "fellowships" that have formed as a result of his false teachings.

■ The Big Question

> Now the big question. What are we to do now that we have this information concerning the church? (*sic*)
> If the church age has come to an end, what are the believers to do who are members of churches? (*sic*)

Camping concludes by raising the "big issue." If what he has been saying is true, what are his followers to do? Here Camping sheds all form of pretense and blatantly seeks to remove the sheep from the fold right under the nose of the shepherds. How are people to put into practice the results of his teachings? He offers some suggestions:

Obedience to the command of Luke 21:20–24 can be accomplished in various ways. If a person or family is a member of a church they can withdraw their membership and fellowship on Sundays with whomever there may be who are of like mind. Such withdrawal may initiate a move by the church to excommunicate. For that individual that is not a trauma because he has become convinced that the church era has come to an end and the church no longer has any divine authority.

The arrogance that resonates in these words is simply shocking. Given the ridiculous forms of argumentation used up to this point, to treat the proper and necessary discipline of the church in this fashion is simply blasphemous. What a burden Harold Camping will bear for this kind of teaching! A person may well become convinced by Camping's smooth speech, but such a person will not be able to shift the burden of their responsibility onto Camping! The Word warns us to take care lest we be led astray, and Harold Camping is one of many voices seeking to lead men and women astray. And remember, if the church no longer has divine authority, *who does?* Seemingly, Family Radio and the "fellowships" formed by the teaching of Harold Camping, who then look to *him* for guidance! Woe to the one who so blatantly seeks to draw away the disciples after himself!

If the individual or family are simply attending a church and are not members they can stop attending that church but continue to fellowship outside of the church with individuals of like mind.

Not under divine authority now? Stay that way! Remain in soul-danger!

If a congregation decides to be obedient to this command they can reorganize their congregation from a church congregation, to become a fellowship of believers. The elders will no longer be elders. The deacons will no longer be deacons. The Pastor will no longer be pastor. In other words no individuals will have spiritual rule over the congregation.

In other words, spiritual anarchy will ensue that results in an unworkable, unguided conglomeration of confused individuals; no spiritual authority will exist at all, no oversight will be available. Service (as promoted by the deaconate) will end. Discipline will collapse, doctrine will erode, and the name of Christ will be slandered, for His own divine wisdom in establishing the church and ordering it has been rejected in favor of the unbiblical speculations and meandering thoughts of a single radio teacher from California.

Dangerous Airwaves: Camping Teaches on Family Radio

In the previous chapter we examined the written presentation offered by Harold Camping regarding his teaching on the end of the church age. In this chapter, and the one that follows, we examine his *spoken* teachings, for Camping is, first and foremost, a radio teacher. Some of the themes he strikes in the following study appeared in the written material, of course, but other elements did not. The first section of Camping's teaching appeared in "Family Radio's Family Bible Study, Based Upon Hebrews 11:34, A Study on Hezekiah, Part 59, Lesson #883," aired in August of 2001. The second section is derived from quotations from Camping's presentation of his new doctrine in the thirteen-part series, "The End of the Church Age" which was presented on Family Radio and then posted on the Family Radio website.

■ The Hebrews Bible Study
One of the first full presentations of this new teaching I encountered came in the form of a "Hebrews" Bible Study from Harold Camping. He speaks of God's "new plan" in these words:

> But in our day, when the population's exploding, God's developed a new plan. And we're seeing more and more of that as we look at this study and as we study some other things in the Bible. And the occasion for this change in plan is that God finally indicates that there comes a time when He will not put up with the false doctrines and the wrong practices that have been part of the New Testament Church all through its history. Even as in the Old Testament we read

about the kings of Judah and each one, many of them, loved the Lord greatly, God blessed them greatly, and yet within their kingdom there were high places. High places is where they worshipped other gods. In other words, where the mind of man prevailed over the mind of God.

The best way to present a radical doctrine is to reveal it very slowly, presenting it not "up front," but piece-by-piece, couched in terms that your prospective audience can understand and accept. This Camping does here. All conservative, Bible-believing, Christian-worldview-holding people would agree with: there is much apostasy in what calls itself "Christendom" today. But we already know where Camping is going to go, and know the proposed solution (radical surgery on the level of decapitation) is too extreme and utterly unwarranted. But his listeners do not yet know this.

And that is the church age of 1900 years, Satan is loosed, and so Sennacharib was loosed [Camping says Sennacharib was a "picture of Satan"]. He was on a roll and he not only conquered the ten tribes to the north, so that they ceased to exist, but he almost completely destroyed Judah, except for a remnant in Jerusalem. And when we tie that in to our time we find that God goes along to a certain point in history and then he looses Satan to bring judgment on the church and virtually silences the gospel, the true gospel, within churches.

This means, of course, that any time the Bible records any kind of military action by a godless nation against Israel, it is liable to become a picture of the destruction of the church. Is that really what the Bible is communicating? No, but this does not stop Harold Camping from seeing in every opponent of Israel a picture of God's judgment on the church. Has anything changed so that for once we are given a *reason* for the "tie in" that Camping proposes? No, the *modus operandi* remains the same, and we have another incident of *Solus Campingus*: the only basis upon which this "tie" is based is the authority of Harold Camping.

In this passage, Camping says it is Satan who brings judgment on the church. Can one imagine the Lord of the church releasing the enemy of the people of God upon His own body? And we must ask: when did this take place? Was it a process? Or did it happen on a particular day? What marked the event? How was a hard-working elder in Christ's church supposed to know that when he went to bed one night he was a shepherd of God's people, but the next morning he was not? Was the celebration of the Lord's Supper pleasing to God, blessed by His Spirit on December 3, but not on December 4? We are not told. But while most Christians believe the gospel is the power of God, Camping seems to believe it can be driven right out of the very congregations of Christ, and that with God's approval.

> And whatever Satan doesn't conquer, God himself removes the candlestick, because it's a time when God is saying, "No more, no more, there can't be any more of this going on. I've blessed the church, people have become saved," even though there have been wrong doctrines within them, sometimes these doctrines were quite wrong, and yet God blessed the Word of God in these denominations and so the world was evangelized.

Just as Mr. Camping often talks about how God is blessing "ministries like Family Radio" without ever telling us about *any* other such "ministry," he likewise does not get specific as to which churches and denominations he is referring to. It seems clear, however, that he is not even making reference to the more liberal denominations that he would say are in a state of apostasy and have been for a long time. Instead, he is referring to the conservative, Bible-believing, mainly Reformed denominations and congregations in these comments, and claims God removes His Spirit from them in judgment upon the "high places," as we have seen. This is further proven by the fact that Camping says these churches should have "known better:"

> But at the beginning of the final tribulation, now that's the key point. At the beginning of the final tribulation God has a quick change in His action. The beginning of the tribulation signified that the churches have ceased to be the means by which God plans to evangelize the world. And this is why it is great tribulation. Remember in our last study we talked about, it's a time of weeping. It's a time when we

ought to be sorrowing in our hearts because we see the
churches that should have known better, they have not
turned away from their wrong doctrines and so finally God
has removed the candlestick so they have a form of godli-
ness but they really deny the power of it.

The student of the New Testament cannot help but be taken aback
by the use of Paul's description of the *enemies of the church* here
used *of the church itself!* In the following citation Camping again
affirms he is talking about conservative, Bible-based churches when
he even imputes to them a belief in *Sola Scriptura* (a rare enough
belief!):

> The 1900 years when God used the church to evangelize the
> world, with all of its weaknesses, with all of its faults, with
> all of its wrong teachings that are permeated...I'm talking
> about any church that believed the Bible alone and in its en-
> tirety was the Word of God, even though denominations
> varied greatly on such questions as baptism and the Lord's
> table and the nature of salvation and a whole lot of things,
> and yet God used all of these denominations and congrega-
> tions to do, to get on with His work of evangelization. And
> I think we have solid biblical evidence of that.

Yes, and Family Radio grew up and became established and pros-
pered in cooperation with these very churches. The most beloved
programs on the network were those that featured the teaching and
preaching of the ministers of those very denominations.

> But then, God brings that to an end and that signals the be-
> ginning of what the Bible speaks; that there will be great
> tribulation. And its great tribulation because the church has
> been set aside by God as the means by which he's going to
> evangelize the world.

Hopefully the reader has noted already the fact that Camping regularly limits the purpose of the church to mere evangelization, and
there is a reason for this. Camping is setting up Family Radio as the
locus of God's blessings on earth, but there is one problem: Family

Radio cannot do what the church does. The church is so much more than a mere mechanism of evangelism. We saw, in our study of the Bible's teaching on the church, that there is much more to the church than this. The church is the dwelling place of the Spirit, the place of worship, the demonstration of the manifold wisdom of God. Family Radio can be *none* of these things. So if Camping is going to replace the church with Family Radio, he has to *reduce* the church to something that is replaceable. This theme runs throughout his teaching on this subject, and it is reprehensible at best.

> It now has become a hollow shell, even though they still have the Bible there, even though they may still preach from the Bible to some degree, nevertheless there is no power of salvation going on. God has another plan. So, for a few years, for a few years, it is doom and gloom. It is very sad what is going to happen next.

Doom and gloom indeed if you are so unwise as to believe Camping's premature deliverance of the eulogy over the grave of the church! Again the theme of the absence of the Spirit of God is presented. Remember that Camping admits that the Bible is still there; that there is preaching from the Bible going on. So how can he say that where the Bible is preached there is no power of salvation? Because the Spirit has been removed from the Church. The gospel message itself can be proclaimed directly from the pages of the Word of God, and yet the Spirit of God *refuses* to honor that proclamation since it is made within the confines of the church! The gravity of the heresy is only increased by the utter lack of integrity in the arguments used to spawn it.

> If you go back to 2 Kings 20...you'll notice it says, and remember that Hezekiah had been told that right in the prime of his years he is going to die. And this was the same year, he's 39 years old, and it's the same year that Sennacharib is assaulting Jerusalem and almost conquered it, he didn't conquer it, but he did conquer the other cities, and it's a time when Jerusalem is in terrible, terrible trouble. It is at this time that God came to Hezekiah and told him, "You're going to die. Prepare, get your house in order,

you're going to die." And we saw last time that Hezekiah was a picture of God's plan of evangelization. He is a man of God and God is using him as a picture. And so at this point Hezekiah in a real sense is dead. Is dead.

I'm sure even Hezekiah would find Camping's comments most surprising. Hezekiah was not dead, but Camping's willingness to kill off the king of Judah just for the sake of making the "connection" tells us just how far he will go to make his teachings "fit." One cannot help but be reminded of how the Watchtower Bible and Tract Society (Jehovah's Witnesses) is forced to change the entirety of history and teach that Jerusalem fell in 607 B.C. (it fell in 586) just to make their 1914 prophecy "fit." Likewise Camping must massage the historical situation.

> And then we read in v. 4, it came to pass, before Isaiah, in other words Isaiah is a representative of God here, we see here that Hezekiah has been told, "You're gonna die, right now, right now, it's the end," then he pleads with God and then Isaiah leaves him, and before Isaiah was gone out into the middle court... Now that word court is an interesting word. It's city. It's the same word that's used throughout the Bible as city. Before he had come to the middle of the city, the word of the Lord came to him saying, [quotes biblical text]...Alright, now, here we see the life of Hezekiah is going to be a picture of God's closing plan for the earth. He is told he's going to die. That's the way God is telling the churches today at the beginning of the final tribulation. You are no longer being used of me to evangelize the world.

In case you are wondering, "But...Hezekiah didn't die, and yet, Camping is saying the church has been destroyed," do not feel badly. That is the logical thing to consider. But logical considerations are irrelevant to allegorical flights of fancy, and hence are no impediment to Mr. Camping's teaching. Hezekiah is not the church, nor a picture thereof. Camping says we "see" that Hezekiah's life "is going to be a picture of God's closing plan on earth" but this is yet another proclamation of *Solus Campingus*...Harold Camping as the ultimate authority. He announces this, but since he never seems to feel any responsibility to give us a *basis* for the statement, we can only give the assertion the weight we assign to him as an interpreter of the Word.

But this quotation of Camping gives us another reason to question his accuracy as an interpreter of the Bible. He tells us that the word for "court" is actually the word for "city." He goes on to build an entire discussion solely upon this assertion. And yet, why is it that the KJV, NKJV, NASB, NIV, NJB, RSV, NRSV, ESV, NLT, TEV, and even the Roman Catholic NAB and the Jewish TNK, *all* have some form of "court" rather than "city"? The Bible student can readily discover the reason. The Greek Septuagint translation of the Old Testament (commonly called the LXX) contains the reading *aule*, "court." The Hebrew manuscripts likewise contain a textual variant here, reflected in the LXX. As the critical apparatus of the *Biblia Hebraica Stuttgartensia* indicates, the text reading is הָעִיר which means "city," but the "to be read" reading is חָצֵר which means, "court." Scholars of all persuasions (Protestant, Catholic, and Jewish) agree that the best reading, found in Hebrew manuscripts, and in many versions, such as the LXX, is "court." It fits the context best as well. The point of the text is that very quickly the word of the Lord came to Isaiah, before he had even gotten out of the palace itself. Saying the word of the Lord came to him halfway across the city does not fit nearly as well, hence the consistent reading of the Bible translations. Why doesn't Mr. Camping tell his listeners this? We do not know, but given that Mr. Camping is not a Bible scholar, and seems to utilize nothing more in-depth than Strong's Concordance as his source of biblical studies, this alone would explain it: he is unaware of the textual issue here. And if this is the case with this passage, in how many other passages where Mr. Camping *thinks* he is "sure" has he simply not done his homework? Despite this, Camping waxes on eloquently about the "middle of the city":

> And then right at the middle of the city, and that's a very in-
> teresting piece of information because what is the city
> of God ultimately? What is the city of God? It consists of
> all who become believers. We can't prove this of course,
> but it is a fact that approximately, as near as we can tell,
> approximately there were as many people who have lived
> and died up until this time as are presently living in the

world today. In other words, today there are six billion people living in the world, and if the Lord tarries for a little while pretty soon it'll be seven billion, in other words, presently, in our present generation, we can say there are six or seven billion people in the world. We can also say with some speculation that probably about six or seven billion people have lived and died in the previous 13,000 years. So, if God is saving approximately the same percentage of people today as He is back throughout the past 13,000 years, we're at about the half point of the building of the city of God. You see that relationship? We're in the middle of the city of God. Up till this point in time, approximately, we are not exact of course, we can say that about half of the people who are to become saved have become saved. Yet we live in a world of six billion going on toward seven billion people in which most of them have not heard the true gospel, because during the last few years while the population has been exploding, there has been very little sending forth of the true gospel, except for ministries like Family Radio. So we are right at the halfway point at this point in time, because at this point in time, suddenly we are finding that the latter rain is beginning to develop, that God is opening door after door to send the gospel out into the world in order to reach the six or seven billion people that still remain to be evangelized, and He's doing it without the church, it's outside.

The entirety of this presentation collapses if, indeed, the proper reading of the text in question is "court," but even if we take it as "city," anyone can see just how tremendously far Camping is reaching to come up with this entire discussion of the world's population, all so that he can say the latter rains are falling and the church has been done away with!

■ Camping the Numerologist

Harold Camping likes numbers, especially when he can work them into his eschatological schemes. He loves to bring together numbers from all sorts of widely divergent contexts and make great and grandiose conclusions based upon his "insights" into how they fit together. In the following quotation note how he deals with the fact that one of his sources contains a number that simply does not fit:

> Now remember that we saw the two witnesses...lets go back to Revelation 11...and we find there that it says that, first of all, it says that in verse 2, "that the holy city shall they tread under foot forty and two months." Now forty and two months is equivalent to three and a half years. Three and a half years is half of seven. In the Bible seven is the number of perfection. And its interesting that when we look at the typology of the Old Testament, God typifies this final tribulation as a period of seventy years. Now whether it's seven years, or seventy years, or seven hundred years, the number ten or a hundred, just signifies completeness. In other words, seventy years signifies the complete perfection of God's final tribulation that began with the moment when Hezekiah died, it began, when the, when, that is, was supposed to have died, [Hezekiah did not die! An amazing twisting of Scripture!] it began when Jerusalem was as-saulted and almost destroyed, when the ten tribes were de-stroyed...these are all pictures of the time when the begin-ning of that final tribulation did begin. And for three and a half, that is, forty-two months, that is three and a half years, the temple will be trodden under foot. That is, it's not functioning. Because if its trodden under foot it means it can't function as a voice of God. And that's the first part, the first half, of the final tribulation. That same three and a half is emphasized when we looked at the two witnesses. They also, notice, they were killed and their bodies were out in the street...remember the two witnesses are the church as it brings the gospel throughout the New Testa-ment era, and finally when their testimony is completed, we read in Revelation 11, when they shall have finished their testimony, the beast that ascendeth out of the bottom-less pit shall make war against them and shall overcome them and kill them. And their dead bodies shall be in the street of that great city which spiritually is called Sodom and Egypt, where also our Lord was crucified. And they of the people and kindreds and tongues and nations shall see

their dead bodies three days and a half. There again, you notice, three and a half. Forty-two months. Three and a half years. Here it is three and a half days. Look for a moment again at James chapter 5; remember the rain stopped coming down for how long? For how long? It's the same period, we read in v. 17 that it might not rain, and it rained not on the earth by the space of three years and six months. Again you see, a half of seven, a half of seven, a half of seven. Forty-two months, it says, three and a half days, and we see the three and a half years. It's all the same period of time. It's the first part of the final tribulation period. The only language in the Bible that gives any time notice to the first part of the final tribulation that is not three and a half is Daniel 8. Look at that for just a moment. In Daniel 8 we have the same period of time, only there it is addressed with different language. There we read...in verse ten as it's talking about Satan, that he waxed great, even to the host of heaven, and cast down some of the hosts and of the stars to the ground...[citation continues]...and then notice in v. 13...see the parallel language to Revelation where the temple is trodden underfoot for forty-two months. But here it says the time is 2,300 days, then shall the sanctuary be cleansed, that is, the sanctuary again will be made righteous. So this 2300 days of Daniel 8 is the equivalent period of time that is called forty-two months in Revelation 11, it's called three and a half years in James 5, it is called three and a half days in Revelation 11. It is all the same period of time. It is the first part of the final tribulation period. And it immediately follows the moment when God has declared the church now has been judged, it has been found wanting, and it no longer is to be used of God for evangelization purposes. It has come to an end, and that's why there's great weeping as we think about that.

Just in case you do not carry a calculator with you and have suffered through the "new math" like most modern Americans, 2300 days is approximately 6.4 years (76.7 months), not 3.5 years. Yet, utterly undaunted by this, Camping glibly opines, "It is all the same period of time." See? Facts, original meaning, and context: it is all irrelevant. The over-riding thing is the "scheme," the "plan" Harold Camping is promoting. And we can at least say he is consistent in one thing: biblical facts, contexts, history, and meaning—none of this ever gets in the way of the "scheme." *Solus Campingus.*

■ John 21 Misused

No discussion of Camping's alleged "biblical proofs" of his teaching would be complete without at least some reference to the wildly complex, very involved presentation he bases upon John 21. Much of his teaching on the subject over the summer of 2001 at the Family Radio gatherings was based on this passage.[1] And while it would take far too much space to go verse by verse through all the unfounded connections and "pictures" he presents, a few of them should suffice to demonstrate, to the fair minded, anyway, the error of his entire approach.

Camping begins by placing the context of John 21 precisely in the modern day. In essence, no one, until Harold Camping, has understood this passage. One is tempted to wonder how it was that hundreds of generations of Christians have drawn spiritual insight and comfort from the passage in the past, being utterly clueless as to what it was about, but that fact does not at all impede Camping's further progress. For example, since John uses the name "Sea of Tiberias" this tells us that the whole point of John 21 is "worldwide," since this is the Roman designation. There are seven disciples in the boat, and since Mr. Camping has never yet encountered a number he could not read a particular meaning into (every number in Scripture, it seems, has a meaning far beyond the historical facts being narrated), he does the same here, telling us the seven apostles represent the entirety of the church, who are out fishing for men. The boat, then, is the church. He makes sure to tell us that boats can sink, and hence, the church can be destroyed too. This is proven by noting that in Luke 5:2–7, two boats are seen (and two is said to be connected with the church—how we are not told) and when they attempt to bring in the great catch of fishes, they start to sink. This proves the church can be destroyed as well. The fact that the boats did not sink is ignored: the fact that they were only flooding due to God's overwhelming blessing is passed by as well. That's the glory of simply incoherent allegorical interpretation: you can pick only those facts that fit your scheme, and ignore all the ones that do not.

However, while this is what verse two refers to, verse three somehow fast-forwards about 1900 years, for the apostles do not catch anything. Hence, there is some transition taking place, or so we are told. So when verse four comes along, Camping tells us,

> We read in verse 4, Jesus stood on the shore, but the disciples knew not that it was Jesus. Now that's a very negative statement, because this is a picture of the church, and somehow they're not recognizing Jesus. There's a major defect in their understanding of what Jesus is doing, what Jesus' program is. And that exists today, that exists today. You talk to pastor after pastor or church after church, and they have no idea of the latter rain. They have no idea of how a ministry like Family Radio fits into the whole picture of world evangelization. There is a major defect in their thinking. Their eyes have been blinded. And so God is saying they did not see Jesus.

So the fact that the disciples, early in the morning, did not recognize Jesus on the shore (how surprising is this, since they surely were not expecting a visit from Him?) is meant to indicate that there is something wrong with the church now in this story. In fact, due to the fact that the majority of pastors do not understand Camping's doctrine of "the latter rain" nor the seeming centrality of Family Radio in God's plans, this amounts to a problem in seeing what Jesus is doing, what His "program" is.

But in verse 5 the entire setting changes yet once again. How does Camping know this? Because Jesus refers to the apostles as "little children." This is somehow related to the "latter rains" as well. Then he turns to verse six and focuses strongly upon the phrase "and then they were not able to haul it in." That is, he says that it really should be rendered "no longer able," and hence, since the ship is the church, there comes a time when the catch of fish (i.e., those who are being saved) will "no longer" be able to bring them *into* the ship (hence, salvation will take place *outside* the ship). Notice his own explanation, and how he brings in passages we have already examined and found him to be misusing:

> But now, if we read here "they were no longer, no longer."

The fish were there. These are the ones who typified believers. They were in the net. The ship had cast the net. But they were no longer to be in control of those fish. You see, for over 1900 years God has appointed, this is as I have indicated, the church is a divine organism, appointed by God, ordained by God, with the task of ruling over His program to get the gospel into all the world. That is the way God had established it. That is why churches send out missionaries and that's why they are always careful to make sure they have elders and deacons who have the spiritual rule...they rule over the activities God has assigned to them, and the ultimate assignment was to bring the Gospel so that people would come in and they would come in, make their confession of faith, they would be baptized, they would join the church as members, even though the net broke, as we saw in Luke 5, so that everybody that looks like they came in as a true member might only be wood, hay, and stubble, rather than a precious stone...but amongst all that came in, there were the precious stones, there was the gold, there was the silver, the genuine articles that did come in. But now the church is no longer able to do that. No longer. Why? Why? Because, as we read, go back to Revelation 11, Revelation 11, and there we read, who are the two witnesses? They are the, verse four, the two candlesticks standing before the God of the earth, and hold your finger there and look quickly for a moment at Revelation chapter one, Revelation one, and there we see in Revelation one that the, in verse twenty, the seven stars are the angels of the seven churches, and the seven candlesticks which thou sawest are the seven churches. The candlesticks represent congregations which are sending the gospel out into the world. But then in verse 7, Revelation 11, and when they shall have finished their testimony, the beast that ascended out of the bottomless pit shall make war against them and shall overcome them and kill them. Back in Revelation 13 the beast is Satan who comes out and overcomes them. It is the time when the church has completed the work God had assigned it to do, and now God says your work is finished. He allows the church to be over-run with wrong doctrines and with a gospel that is not totally faithful to the Word of God, and He's through with it. He's through with it. Because their work has been finished, and they "no longer" can bring the fish into the ship. Now the point is...what was the purpose of the ship? The purpose of the ship was to enable the fish who were caught in the net to be brought to shore, to be brought into the kingdom of God. The fish were caught in the net, the gospel, they were put in the ship, which is the church, the congregations, and the ship would take the cargo, this precious cargo, to the seaport, and that was a beautiful picture of the ship being used, the church being used, to bring people into the kingdom of God. The church was there in between as an intermediary between those who were hearing the gospel and Christ Himself. And they received whatever authority they had from God. They were not an authority over God, which they did assume very often. But they had an authority which was received from God so that they might be used of God to bring the gospel. But now they have a great multitude of fish, but they are no longer able to draw it for the multitude of the fish. They're just not able."

This lengthy quote helps the reader who is not familiar with Camping's style get a "taste" for the way in which he weaves together seemingly plausible statements together with (a-contextual) scriptural citations, resulting in a presentation that can confuse the biblically illiterate or those who are easily swayed by arguments that are not, upon examination, meaningful. We have already seen that the main elements of the preceding section collapse upon the most surface-level examination. But what of the key assertion, that what is really said in John 21:6 is that they were "no longer" able to bring in the catch of fish?

First, quite honestly, the point is irrelevant. The boat referenced no longer exists. It was a wooden boat in Galilee and it is long gone. So is the net. So are the fish. This is an historical incident where the Lord appeared to the disciples. It is not a complex secret code unknown to anyone before Harold Camping. One does not need a gnostic-style "knowledge" to figure out how to follow the ever-shifting scene, how one item means this in one verse, but then something else in the next, etc. So let's say we translate it in such a way as the disciples could "no longer" draw the net into the boat. Such makes perfect sense: when it was empty, they could. Now it is filled to overflowing, and the seven of them can't get it into the boat. Such has nothing whatsoever to do with the work of the church at the end of the age: it has to do with Christ's supernatural ability, as a resurrected man, to control nature, just as He did prior to His crucifixion and burial. Jesus remains Lord of Creation: this is the point.

But even here another possibility exists that Camping ignores, and that comes from the imperfect tense of the verb used. As one commentator has expressed it, this refers to the repeated efforts on the part of the disciples to bring in the huge catch of fish. The translation would then be, "they were now not able to draw it."

In either case, the torturous mishandling of John 21 continues from here, building upon itself until it, like the fanciful Marian doctrines of the Roman Catholic Church, builds an edifice of belief upon a pebble of improbability.

The Debate That Almost Was

It took me many years, but I finally convinced my dear friend Chris Arnzen to get a computer. And then I cajoled and hounded and eventually got him to start coming into our "Internet Relay Chat" channel. And so it was that one day we were discussing Harold Camping's teaching when I said, "I would dearly love to hear him actually attempt to exegete such passages as Matthew 16:18 and especially Ephesians 3:20–21." Chris was in channel when I made these comments.

The next afternoon around dinnertime my cell phone rang. It was Chris. "I'm on hold for the Open Forum. Turn on your radio." And so I did, and stood for more than half an hour as Chris asked questions of Mr. Camping. Now as all listeners of the Open Forum know, Mr. Camping takes a call and then turns the caller's volume down while he answers. He may, or may not, turn up the volume again. Often he just goes on to the next caller. But for some reason, in God's providence, this evening Camping kept bringing Mr. Arnzen back up and allowing him to continue to ask probing questions.

It should be noted that Mr. Arnzen has, as of the date of this writing, twice invited Mr. Camping to publicly debate his "new" teaching against James White. The first time we were turned down cold, the second time a small door of opportunity was left open. In either case, we surely feel that the allegorical interpretations of Harold Camping would not survive rigorous cross-examination, which can only be provided, in fairness, in a scholarly debate setting (the Open Forum does not allow for this due to Camping's control of the volume knob). But since Mr. Arnzen asked many of the questions I would want to ask, and since we have the entire call available in transcribed form, I felt it might be useful to provide the call in its entirety, along with commentary that would cast light upon the assertions Camping made that Mr. Arnzen was not allowed to respond to. This call took place December 27, 2001. HC stands for Harold Camping, CA for Chris Arnzen.

■ **Welcome to Open Forum**

HC: Welcome to Open Forum

CA: Hello Mr. Camping

HC: Yes...

CA: I have a two-part question for you basically. The first part would be, when you started out some months ago telling the listeners that Christ was through with the Church you were somewhat more hesitant and not completely certain of it, and later you seem to now be very certain of it to the point you're telling people to leave their churches, and I wanted to also ask you on top of that your interpretation of Ephesians 3:21 which says "To Him be glory in the church by Christ Jesus throughout all ages world without end." If you could comment on both of those I would appreciated it.

Mr. Arnzen presented two excellent questions, both striking at the heart of Camping's teaching. The first demonstrates the danger already noted in this teaching: that it has taken on the nature of on-going revelation, new "insights" never before seen. The second presents a biblical passage that, as we have seen, when it is properly exegeted clearly points to the on-going nature of Christ's church. If this were all Mr. Arnzen had been able to get on the air, it would have been worth the call. But as we will see, it was not the end of the interaction at all.

HC: Well, yes in Ephesians chapter three, you know, there's one principle that we have to keep in mind, and that is, when God talks about the church, there are two possibilities. When He talks about the church in...Revelation 2 or Revelation 3, the church in Ephesus or the Church in

Laodicea, He's talking about the external corporate body, the visible church which is made up both of believers and non-believers. And it has no guarantee. We already read in Revelation 2 and 3 where God warned the Church in Ephesus—If you don't straighten up and return to your first love, I'll remove your candlestick, and to have their candlestick removed would mean that they would become a dead church. He already warned the church at Sardis "You are dead, you are dead, even though you have some believers within you, you're already a dead church." Now that's the corporate body, the external body. But God also talks about the church from...about the church that is invisible, eternal in character, and it is only made up of those who have become true believers. And that's what Ephesians chapter 3 and verse 10 is talking about, that to the intent now, unto the principalities and powers in heavenly places might be known by the church the manifold wisdom of God, that is the, the body of believers, those who have truly become saved. Here the word church is used like God uses it in Matthew chapter 16, "I will build my church, and the gates of hell shall not prevail against it." That can only be speaking about the invisible, eternal church that is no longer, those people no longer are threatened by hell because their sins have all been paid for. Now unfortunately, theologians don't distinguish between these two. It's amazing. I've received a number of letters from pastors in recent weeks, and invariably they go to Matthew 16 and say "You see, Christ will build His church, and the gates of hell shall not prevail against it." They have no understanding that that is not talking about the corporate body, the external body. They had...they aren't thinking about the fact that the churches in...the seven churches in Revelation all disappeared in time, that...because they became apostate. They don't realize that that's talking about the invisible, eternal church.

We have already addressed the slight-of-hand that Mr. Camping is using here: noting the fact that no single congregation of Christ's church is promised never-ending existence (witness all the churches that disappeared, not due to "high places," but due to being over-run by the advance of Islam in the seventh century) is a non-disputed fact of history and experience. But Camping expands this simple truth into a completely different realm when he takes this to mean that the entirety of the visible church, every congregation, every assembly, can be destroyed *at the same time.* This is a completely invalid conclusion drawn from insufficient grounds. The church subsists in each and every one of those true congregations, so that her existence on earth is not ended when any particular organized body comes to an end.

To speak of the "invisible" church is to speak in the broadest possible categories of the church as an entire entity. But to claim that the invisible church is indestructible while at the same time proclaiming the death, or destruction, or end of the church on earth, is to engage in the grossest form of self-contradiction and equivocation. As we saw in our exposition of the biblical teaching on the church, it is Christ's will that the church exist in a particular form, and that the Father receive glory through the life and ministry of the *visible* church.

So Mr. Camping is not only in error when he says that "theologians" ignore the issue of the visible and invisible church (surely anyone who has read even the most basic works on the church knows better), but he is in error to glibly assert that the defectibility of a single congregation, or even a group thereof, implies the possibility of the destruction of the entirety of the visible church of Christ on earth.

> Now incidentally you noted that as time is going I become more and more firm in this conviction that we're at that time, and that is true. It's based on more and more evidence piling up from the scriptures. This is not something that is talked about in an incidental manner. As a matter of fact...I'm getting calls, I'm getting letters, I'm getting information from all kinds of people who are ahead of me, they are saying "and what about this and what..." They're seeing things that I haven't even seen. Corroborating the fact that indeed that is what the Bible is teaching—we're at that time in history, and that the church now is under the judgment of God and it's the beginning of the end. It's the hour of judgment that the Bible talks about that's going on right

> now. And it's the judgment on the churches and congrega-
> tions because they have not removed their high places and
> because their work has been finished. God...God's work is
> not frustrated.... He's used the churches for over 1900
> years and their work now has been finished and...God has
> used it...the churches very successfully for over 1900 years.

These words are very troubling. This means that Camping's followers, freed from the constraints of sound biblical exegesis, are running ahead of him and "seeing" in this passage or that the same
"truths" he has been explaining. Of course, whether Camping will
accept all of these "insights" or not is problematic: allegorical interpretation exists primarily in the mind of the reader and has nothing
to do, really, with the text as it was written. Camping may not "like"
what some of his followers are "seeing" and he is surely under no
constraint to accept their insights (just as no one else need put an
ounce of weight into his own ruminations). But the fact he can ex-
press himself in the context of evidence "piling up" (hasn't it *always*
been there, if revelation is completed?) and "seeing" things that even
Camping has not "seen" takes us to the very border of new revelation itself. Every aberrant religious movement has begun with some
teacher who has elevated his own "insights" to just this kind of sta-
tus. It is truly a dangerous thing we see here in Camping's words.

■ Should We Flee the Churches?

> CA: Should we leave the congregations that we're members
> of?

> HC: Well now, let me ask you the question. If God the Holy
> Spirit is not operating in your midst, and the Bible teaches
> that, so that regardless of how well your pastor is preach-
> ing, no one is becoming saved, would you really want to be
> in that congregation with your family?

This is truly an incredible assertion on the part of a man who is obviously presenting nothing more than the personal (and ungrounded)
"insights" he thinks he has as if they were God's truth itself! To limit
the work of the Holy Spirit so as to insist, based upon your own wild
speculations, that He can no longer save His people when He wills

and where He wills is simply astounding! Note Camping's repeated assertion, "and the Bible teaches that...." This is his standard terminology for "my allegorical interpretations." Sadly, his followers equate his interpretations with the Word itself. The Bible nowhere supports the idea that the Holy Spirit of God will abandon the Bride of Christ; allow her to be destroyed by Satan, so that He will only save His elect *outside* of the church.[1] Nowhere do we get direct, plain teaching indicating that a man of God can preach the Word effectively and clearly and yet the Holy Spirit of God will *refuse* to honor that proclamation and draw the elect unto salvation. This kind of amazing assertion requires far more than the convoluted allegorical "types" and "pictures" offered by Mr. Camping in support of it.

CA: Why do you think nobody is being saved in my church when we see people coming to Christ almost every month?

HC: Well now, what...how do we define "people coming to Christ?" How do we define that? You know there's a great number who...believe they're becoming saved because they...excuse me, we'll talk about this in just a min...after this message. [Break] You know, people belong to churches and they are convinced that God is really working because...look at the people who have accepted Christ during this past month. But the question is, did they truly become saved? What is the nature of salvation? Is it that I have accepted Christ? No, the Bible doesn't teach that. The Bible teaches to become saved means that God has made me a new creature. He's given me a brand new resurrected soul. In which, and it means that God has accepted me. It isn't something that I can trigger. I can't decide when I'm going to become saved, because...there's no way that I'm in charge of that. It is God who has to do the whole work of salvation. But we're living in a day of the works-grace gospel. Virtually every denomination has doctrines in which they teach that, yes, Christ saves us by His Grace, but we have to do something. We have to have faith, or we have to reach out and accept Him, or we have to get baptized in water, and so on. And actually that's reprehensible to God

because salvation is entirely the work of grace. There's no
way that we can make any contribution.

In a real cross-examination, Mr. Camping would not fare well at this
point. In fact, throughout the exchange, the answers given to the
specific questions are often "non-responsive" in the formal sense of
the phrase. Any problems the church may have in truly determining
the reality of a person's conversion do not disappear in Mr. Camping's position.[2] We have already noted the listing of "high places"
that Mr. Camping gives, and that *some* of those concepts have at
least elements of truth in them. But here Camping seemingly paints
with a very broad brush, for he lumps together the teachings of all of
evangelicalism, conservative or liberal, Reformed or Arminian. He
then throws in his strange and unbalanced concept that denies faith
the instrumental function the Bible clearly gives it,[3] and the result is
a blanket indictment of all of evangelicalism.

At this point Camping went into a long discussion of an evange-
listic rally he once participated in, and how very few people actually
came to know Christ as a result of this massive effort. He then
continues,

> And so, you know the Bible talks about that, and it indi-
> cates that—particularly in our day, if the Holy Spirit is not
> working there, we can have all the outward evidence, like at
> this crusade I was talking about, but that doesn't mean that
> there is salvation, and we have to listen to what God says.
> And God says that this is...that it's outside. That there's a
> great multitude which no man can number that are being
> saved. I firmly believe that. Wherever the whole counsel of
> God is being brought and where it's outside, I believe that
> there are a great many people becoming saved, because I
> trust the Bible. I don't know who they are. I don't know
> where they are. I will never meet them. But I know it's hap-
> pening. Because God says so, and that's all that's important.

Camping repeats his utterly unfounded assertion that the Holy Spirit is somehow limited from working within the church, and uses this
then to assert that even if we see conversions, they are not really conversions, since salvation is only taking place "outside" the church!

Remember that this entire argument is built upon seeing a boat in John 21 as a picture of the church, and the net filled with fishes not being able to be brought into the boat. We often chide Roman Catholics for basing entire dogmas upon short phrases or verses like "You are blessed among women" and "Son, behold your mother." Yet here we have Mr. Camping turning the entire doctrine of the work of the Spirit, the church, the proclamation of the gospel, etc., upside down, and on what basis? Disjointed allegorical "pictures" compiled without the first concern for context or meaning.

And again we sound the note of alarm: Camping's allegorical "insights" have become to him the very utterance of God. He says "and God says that this is…that it's outside." God has never said any such thing. God revealed that Jesus had supernatural control over fish in His resurrected body and directed the Apostles to them when they were fishing. Period! To extrapolate this story out to this level is simply ridiculous. He assures us that where the "full counsel of God" is being proclaimed, *as long as it is outside the church,* salvation is taking place. And where is the full counsel of God heard? Only on Family Radio, it seems. Camping says "God has said so," but in reality, Camping has said so; and he dares to equate his context-less conclusions about pictures and symbols with the very speech of God!

■ The Shoe on the Other Foot

> CA: …also many people who listen to Family Radio who think they got saved but turned out to be false converts as well and fell away? I mean, I agree with you that it's a dangerous thing that the Arminian churches are doing, to think people are saved just by going forward in an altar call, but I don't believe that. I've been a member of a Reformed congregation that strongly believes in the doctrines of Grace. But having said that, do you think that also that there are thousands of Family Radio listeners who can also turn out to be false converts?

> HC: Well, but you see, the problem is that if they're listeners to Family Radio…in order to be an intense listener you have to be ready to accept a lot of things that you're not getting in your churches. In Family Radio you hear that when

you become saved you become a brand new person. You
receive a brand new resurrected soul. You don't hear that in
the churches. If you're listening to Family Radio, you hear
that we cannot...trust in...that faith is a instrument that
brings us to Christ. We can't accept the idea that baptism is
a...seal of any kind and you don't hear that in churches. In
other words you have to have a different mindset to be an
avid listener to Family Radio. As a matter of fact, in most
churches, if you are an avid listener to family radio, they
would really wish you weren't there.

We note in passing that this section truly reveals Camping's understanding of the adversarial relationship that not only exists now, as a
result of his new attacks upon Christ's church, but that has existed
for quite some time. He goes back to some of the unique elements *of
his own personal theology*, identifies them as *constituent elements of
the gospel itself*, and then, upon this basis, insists that those who are
"avid" listeners to Family Radio show their true state of conversion
by their willingness to listen to, and accept, *his teachings! Sola
Harold Camping* might well be the phrase used to describe this kind
of thinking!

There are exceptions, there are churches that are exceptions, but in most churches they wish you weren't there because you're always troubled with some of the things you're
hearing from the pulpit. You hear that we have to stand at
the judgment throne, or you hear that you have to do this in
order to become saved, or whatever, and then there are
questions that are raised, and so...this is one of the reasons
that in many churches Family Radio is a bad name and
there are pastors who say, tell their congregation, "Don't
listen to the Open Forum whatever you do" because they...
you're gonna be hearing things that are unacceptable. This
is par for the course in our day.

And yet this is not an answer to the question Mr. Arnzen asked.
There truly is no answer, for Mr. Camping's position is just as liable
to criticism as the one he is attempting to undermine. He may use his
allegories to deny the Spirit a place in the church, but upon what

basis does he then provide a *positive* teaching regarding the role of the Spirit now in his new "fellowships"? How can he substantiate the idea that there are thousands being saved in the ministry of Family Radio when he denies the reality of the salvation of those who hear the gospel in the church? His teaching is a two-edged sword, but he doesn't seem to see the blade cuts in both directions.

CA: ...Family Radio still airs sermons of local pastors without, of course, telling the listeners that they are pastors. You still use the sermons of Godly pastors all over the country in your different broadcasts. You still use them...

HC: Well, but first of all, first of all we have permission from those pastors to do this, and they're not being aired as church...as given from a church, they're just from...we trust they are believers who are...and we listen to them very carefully to make sure that they are altogether faithful to the Word of God. We're being exceedingly careful that we teach faithfully from the Bible, and many, many, many messages that we could air we cannot air because they're not as faithful as they should be. And so we are trying to be a ministry that is...and we never have been a church, we are not a church, we're not a para-church. We don't ever offer water baptism or offer communion. We don't have a membership. We are simply stewards of the Gospel, we simply share the gospel, and trust that God will do all the work of saving. We don't have to do...any of the work of saving. And when you say you're in your church there are many people that are coming to Christ, well, how do you know? How do you know that they are truly becoming saved? I've served as an elder many, many years. I've heard many testimonies of people who have come before the consistory in order that they might become members and I've seen all kinds of failures in this where you thought...they were able to speak well or they were charming or whatever. And so, yes, it looks like you are a child of God and yet the evidence showed up a few years later...they were not at all. And so you...if you're saying that all kinds of people are becoming saved, what are you looking at, what are you seeing that they've become saved?

Surely all elders have seen people come into congregations with glowing testimonies and yet then prove to be false. The Apostles experienced this in their own ministries, and yet Camping can hardly assert that it was due to "high places" or "the church age having ended"! And what is more, his new "fellowships" will be *more* liable to such things as they lack God-given officers! So we might well turn Mr. Camping's question around and ask him how *he* knows that these great multitudes to which he refers, who are allegedly being saved by the ministry of Family Radio, are in fact made up of truly regenerate individuals? Does he truly dare to say that their willingness to swallow his every word is the criteria? Mr. Arnzen pressed the point masterfully:

> CA: [First part cut off: *They have forsaken* (assumed words)]...wickedness, that they've clung to Christ by His grace and mercy, that they are living lives starkly opposed to the lives they used to lead when they were slaves to sin...
>
> HC: Well but...
>
> CA: They love God....

Arnzen pushes the truth into the forefront. What are the marks of a regenerate person? Forsaking wickedness, clinging to Christ, living Godly lives, showing love for God. Surely this is how the work of the Spirit is recognized, not by a person's willingness to sit transfixed before a radio and believe everything Harold Camping says! Camping has no substantive answer, as his comments reveal:

> HC: Well it's true that God has used the church and there are many many true believers in the church. They can't lose their salvation. And they still may be there...but we're talking about...as the gospel is presented today if the Holy Spirit is not operating there's no one becoming saved.

This is not an answer; it is a case of special pleading. It acknowledges the truthfulness of the question, but then avoids its weight by simply repeating the position Camping is espousing. The evidence of regeneration is in how these people behave: Camping's thesis involves the denial of the presence of the Holy Spirit in the church today. But if people are clinging to Christ and loving God and repenting of sin, how can this be? Do natural men, devoid of the Spirit, do this kind of thing? Of course not! Even Camping's theology would preclude this. So, the question refutes his position, but he refuses to address this directly. Instead, he just repeats, as a mantra, the assertion that the Spirit is no longer in the churches.

> What about our children that are coming along? What about those babies that we're so concerned about for their salvation? It's just like when Jesus...this is not an impossible phenomenon you know...when Jesus preached the Gospel he was the perfect preacher. He preached for three and a half years. Virtually nobody became saved after three and a half years. There are 120 in the upper room and a little more than 500 in all of Galilee. That's after 3 and a half years with a perfect preacher preaching all day long, day after day after day. And then when the Holy Spirit was poured out at Pentecost in one afternoon there was about three thousand who are saved. What's the difference? The fact is that the Holy Spirit was not applying the Word of God that Jesus was preaching to the hearts of any...or... very, very few people.

No one is arguing that the Holy Spirit's work is not necessary for the preaching of the gospel to bring about salvation. Everyone agrees with this. No one (including Mr. Arnzen) is arguing that the quality of the preacher determines the results. It is always a matter of the Spirit's mighty power to remove hearts of stone and give hearts of flesh.

> And if during the church age of over 1900 years God did apply the Word of God to the hearts of people so that even churches that had very bad doctrine were still being used of the Lord to evangelize in the world in wonderful ways. But if the Holy Spirit is not operating, then you could have the most ideal preacher you could name and nobody is becoming saved.

This is not the point of the question, either. Everyone agrees with this statement. The question was designed to show that the Spirit *is* in the church, doing what He has always done, ministering to the saints and bringing the elect unto salvation at the time and in the way the Father has chosen.[4]

> Would you want to, do you want to be there? Now Jesus said very plainly in Luke 21, when you see Jerusalem surrounded by armies...and the only Jerusalem we can talk about are the corporate body...we can't...it's not talking about the Jerusalem above, the true believers, because we can't escape that Jerusalem, we're eternally there. We're eternal citizens of the spiritual, heavenly Jerusalem. And it's not talking about the literal Jerusalem over there alongside the Mediterranean Sea, because that has nothing to do with the whole Christian...the whole Bible...emphasis of our day.... So what other Jerusalem is there? It's the corporate body, the external body of churches and congregations that God is talking about....

This is an amazing statement that violates every canon of meaningful biblical interpretation. The Jerusalem being discussed was the Jerusalem of the original context! Why does Camping reject this? Because it is not centered upon him, his time, and his geographical location! As he admits, "because that has nothing to do with the whole...emphasis of our day." And who determines this "emphasis"? Harold Camping, of course. So the original context is to be ignored simply because it does not fit into what he *wants* the text to say. These words had a clear and obvious meaning when Luke wrote them. In a few short decades the Lord's prophecies about the destruction of Jerusalem were fulfilled when Titus and the Roman legions surrounded Jerusalem and destroyed it. Christians who remembered, and heeded, Jesus' words found safety. What does this have to do with us today? We can learn from this Jesus' knowledge of future events, the fact that Christian worship is not centered in the historical city of Jerusalem, and the Lord's concern for His people. We can speak of God's judgment upon Jerusalem for its rejection of the Messiah, and His righteousness in bringing judgment to bear. All these things are perfectly valid lessons we can learn. But to ignore these things, as Camping does, is a classic example of eisegesis.

> ...and when you see Jerusalem surrounded by armies, let those who are in Judea flee to the mountains, and that's a figure of speech "flee to Christ" and then it says "and those who are within her, depart out." Now that's a plain command that God is giving, and why does He give that command?

First, upon what basis are we to accept the assertion that "flee to the mountains" is a "figure of speech" for "flee to Christ?" This is yet another of the literally hundreds of unfounded *Solus Campingus* statements that fill his every Bible study and Open Forum program. Next, everyone wants to obey God's plain commands. And it is surely a plain command to depart out of Jerusalem when the armies are seen surrounding her. But it is Camping's amazing leap of allegorical fiction that leads us to believe the church is here spoken of rather than the historical Jerusalem that was, of course, surrounded by Titus and the Romans. No matter what else a person may do with these words (let alone those that precede and follow it), their original intention and meaning must be determined first and foremost, and that meaning does not in any fashion support Camping's teaching that this is a command to flee the churches.

> For the security of the true believers. Because, who wants to be in a church that's under the judgment of God? Who wants to be there if the Holy Spirit is not working? Who wants to be there if it is Satan now who has taken his seat in the temple, as we read in 2 Thessalonians 2. These are ugly things. These are traumatic things. These are terrible things that I'm talking about. And yet, I'm quoting from the Bible...I'm not...these aren't ideas that come out of mind... these...I'm quoting from the Bible. This is what God has written about.

One can quote from the Bible continuously and never once speak the truth *as long as the original context and intention is ignored*. And that is what is going on here. Surely Camping quotes Scripture. Who doesn't? But you cannot possibly claim the authority of Scripture if you do not allow it to speak for itself, and Camping's incessant allegorization of the text removes his conclusions from the realm of biblical teaching.

> And when He speaks in the book of James in Chapter 4, "Ye adulterers and adulteresses," He's speaking to the corporate body—the churches and congregations. And if we are holding doctrines...and with almost no exception every church has doctrines that are...contrary to the Word of God...that is spiritual adultery, and that's reprehensible to God. We've come to a time where God won't countenance that any more. He now has said "Alright, your work is finished, and now you're under judgment." And He's warning the true believers "Get out, get out," because you don't want to be part of that judgment.

Of course James spoke to a Christian congregation in his epistle, but as any exegesis of the text reveals, he recognized it was a mixed congregation, including some who were false professors. Many of his exhortations would not apply to *every* person in the congregation, and, in fact, applied to a congregation *in the days of the apostles themselves.* Hence, it obviously has nothing to do with the "end of the church age." Surely sub-biblical teaching is reprehensible to God (which is why we are constantly exhorted to handle correctly the word of God and to seek diligently to bring our faith into conformity with that revelation), but God's way of correcting the church is through *reformation* not through *destruction!*

■ Proclaim the Lord's Death Until He Comes

Another one of the topics of conversation that had come up in our chat channel was Camping's view of the ordinances of the church, especially in light of 1 Corinthians 11:26. This question brought a fascinating response from Camping:

> CA: Are you also teaching that the ordinances of the church are no longer in existence...when people meet in their homes to listen to Family Radio should they not have the Lord's Table and not baptize new believers?

HC: The Lord's table and baptism are ceremonial laws, incidentally. I was never taught that, that they were ceremonial laws. I'd been in a church for eighty years. I'd been taught that they were sacraments. And everybody is taught they're sacraments. The Bible doesn't call them sacraments. There's an implication there and...the confessions...if you search the confessions...I don't care what church you belong to, what your church confesses concerning those ordinances, those ceremonial laws, you'll find that they put more into it, way more than the Bible will allow. They are signs, they are shadows that are...God uses to point us to the Lord's death until He comes and emphasize that we are a communion of believers. But they have no spiritual substance in them. And God, if He has destroyed the church, He's brought the church under judgment...well then, that's where they are to be carried out. They were given to the church throughout the church age. They have served the church in assisting and instructing what the gospel is, but if you are outside of the church you can't use those any more....

Upon what possible basis does Harold Camping assert that the ordinances of Christ's church are "ceremonial laws"? One might argue, if established usage means nothing, that any command that has reference to any religious action or activity could be called a "ceremonial law," but the phrase itself has a long and established meaning. Ceremonial law under the Old Covenant is differentiated from the moral law, and speaks mainly to those actions and activities that set the Jewish people apart and provided types and shadows of the coming Messiah. That is how most people would understand the phrase "ceremonial law," and surely, the ordinances of the Lord's Supper and baptism do *not* fall into that category. They are commands given by Christ to His church. The Supper, especially, is a picture of Christ's death, with the elements representing His flesh and blood. Unlike the types and shadows that looked *forward* to a future fulfillment, the Supper reminds us of a completed act. It is the great privilege of all believers to celebrate the Supper in the fellowship of the Church. And it is a travesty of grand proportions that any believer could be deprived of this blessing through the

ridiculously inconsistent spiritualizations of an unstable[5] teacher
who refuses to allow the Word to speak for itself.

> any more than ancient Israel when they were driven out of
> Jerusalem when the Babylonians destroyed them, they
> couldn't observe the ceremonial laws of burnt offerings and
> blood sacrifices and all of these things because they were
> driven into…they were sent to Babylon to be captives there.
> But God is the one who terminated it, the church didn't.
> God did. And today…we're not terminating these things.
> God has terminated these things. And we simply now have
> the Word of God and we have no ceremonial laws to assist
> us. We can read about them in the Word of God and receive
> spiritual edification from it as we read about it. But insofar
> as observing it, that has to be under the rules of the church
> that God had so carefully established.

Camping seems sensitive to the assertion that he, by his teachings, is
"terminating" the ordinances, and yet, of course, that's exactly what
he is doing, at least for those who follow his teachings. We understand it is his claim that Scripture forces his teachings upon him, but
since this is manifestly not the case, he cannot, by this evasion, free
himself from the weight of responsibility.

It is amazing that Camping then asserts that in the period after
the destruction of the church (the "fellowship" age, perhaps?) believers can "read about them [the ordinances] and receive spiritual
edification from it as we read about it." Can such a notion be enter-
tained for even a moment? Imagine it! Those who once experienced
the glorious *anamnesis,* the act of remembrance of the once-for-all
sacrifice of Jesus Christ upon Calvary, who partook of the bread,
drank of the cup, sang the hymns and proclaimed the Lord's death
"until He comes," now are reduced to reading about what they once
possessed and enjoyed. But now they are deprived of these things
based upon the singular spiritual "insights" of a radio teacher from
California? How is it in any way edifying to read about a greater
privilege held by previous generations of believers? How is it edifying to be reminded that a beautiful and poignant means of proclaiming the Lord's death, one instituted personally by the Lord Himself
prior to His sacrifice, is no longer available to you? That *you* are

restricted from this glorious time of remembrance? It is very hard to take such an assertion seriously.

> The corporate body was not just any old body of people. It was a divine institution that God had established and given very careful rules for the spiritual oversight of that congregation—for the membership of that congregation, the character of the elders and the deacons. The Bible has a lot to say about the character of that institution. But now its come to an end. Its work has been finished. It's under judgment. And so we have to leave it with all of its...with all of the activity that it had been previously involved in, and the only rule that God gives us, first of all, the rule of the Sunday Sabbath hasn't changed. It still is God's holy day. It's a day for worship, for fellowship, for Bible study, for all of these spiritual things.

Camping rightly says the church was (and is) a divine institution. It is interesting that when looking at what the Word says about the church as an institution, Camping does not engage in his allegorization. But when he comes to those passages that speak of its perpetuity, he does.

But, he then says the Sunday Sabbath remains binding in the new age of the non-church "fellowship." This raises the entire issue of just how the "fellowships" that Camping's teachings have spawned are to function. Many are looking to him for guidance at this point, for obvious reasons. The Bible knows nothing of "fellowships," hence, there is no divine guidance as to how these leaderless, formless, organization-less bodies are to function. Since it is Camping's teachings that have led to the development of these "fellowships," he is obviously the one to whom people will turn for instruction. The fact that he cannot turn to Scripture for answers should be more than enough warning to anyone that he has transgressed the boundaries of God's truth.

> Secondly God says don't neglect the assembling of ourselves together, especially as the day draws nigh. So as much as possible we ought to try to find others of like mind who we can fellowship with and...but we're not going to be a

church. We aren't going to have elders and deacons and the
so-called sacraments and so on. We're just going to be a fellowship, and we have one purpose. That purpose is the
same purpose that had been given the church. Go ye into all
the world with the gospel, and which God had used the
church for over 1900 years.

Camping continues to cite Hebrews 10:25 regarding the gathering
of believers despite the fact that it is simply inarguable from a
contextual point of view that the passage was originally written
about gathering together *in the fellowship of the church*. This is a
command Harold Camping is not only violating personally, but is
teaching others to violate as well, despite his continued citation of
the passage.

He then says that the purpose of the "fellowships" is the same as
that of the church. Well, then does it follow that these fellowships
are all pure and have no high places? How could that be, unless they
all walk lock step with him, since he alone seemingly has the ability
to define what the "high places" are? And just how is the mandate to
spread the gospel fulfilled by gathering in fellowships and listening
to a radio? Camping goes on to talk about the massive explosion in
the world's population (one of his pet arguments against the contin-
uation of the church, as if the church cannot, and does not, use the
same technologies that Family Radio does), and yet, how can little
fellowships gathered around radios without guidance, leadership,
or organization, evangelize the world?

But now with people coming on the scene at the rate of
about 10,000 every hour of every day—additional people
added to the population, there's no group of churches that
could minister to that, but God has raised ministries, and
has raised individuals outside of the church to minister to
them and that's the way He's reaching the world and so that
is the big mandate to those who have been driven out of the
churches. The big task is get on with the task of getting the
gospel out into the world and, isn't it marvelous that God is
saving left and right because that's what He says He's doing,
so we know it's true.

But how do pointing men and women to unorganized fellowships accomplish this?

> CA: You quoted just before 1 Cor. 11:26 where you quoted part of the verse where "For as often as you eat this bread and drink this cup , you proclaim the Lord's death till He comes."
>
> HC: Yes...
>
> CA: Aren't we supposed to be doing that until He comes?
>
> HC: Well, that would be ideal. But so were the Old Testament believers to observe the sacrifices continually until Christ would come. They were never to let that fire go out. Read...in Leviticus beginning in chapter 6 verse 12. They were never to let the candlestick go out. These things were to go on continually. But God interrupted it because they...He came to a time when He removed the high places and He brought judgment on them. God interrupted it. And that's exactly parallel, exactly parallel to what has happened to the Churches. God has given those, until I...until He comes and that was simply to indicate that...we're also to look at the completion of our salvation, but God has interrupted that because He's brought judgment upon the church. And so you can't continue when you're under judgment.

This is quite true, but the covenant given to Israel had always had blessings and cursings in it, and God had told the people that if they adopted the ways of the peoples around them they would experience judgment (Deuteronomy 28). But the statement concerning the offerings on the altar is a command to the Jewish people; the words of Paul are written to the church. The problem with Camping's response is that he is inserting his utterly extra-biblical concept of the "end" of the church into the mix. Any person simply listening to Paul's statement would come away with only one conclusion: Paul believed the church of Jesus Christ would be in existence, proclaiming His death, until the Lord Himself returned to earth! This is what Christians have always believed, and Camping has separated himself from *everyone* by thinking otherwise.

CA: ...in the Old Testament ceremonies, the Lord Jesus did come, He actually did come and that abolished the old....

HC: Oh excuse me, in 587 the Lord had not come. He didn't come until 587 years later. But the ceremonies were all stopped cold. The temple was destroyed. The Holy of Holies was gone. The altar was gone. We don't read of any priesthood in Babylon where they were to go and pray for the welfare of the country and where they were to have families and so on. They were to live there in Babylon. They were, they were totally deprived of all of the ceremonies because they all focused on the temple, and the temple was destroyed. And that was 500 years before Christ came.

However, the temple worship *was* going on at the time of the coming of Christ. No one will argue against the fact that God was faithful to His promise to bring judgment against Israel, nor that this involved the interruption of the temple sacrifices. But it is Camping's insistence upon equating anything God did with Israel to the church that is in error: is there no New Covenant? Is there no difference in how God works with the Body of Christ?

■ Is It Slightly Possible, Mr. Camping?

CA: Don't you think that there's even the slightest possibility that you might be causing people to sin by leaving their churches, I mean that there's a slight possibility that you're wrong about Christ being through with the church....

HC: Well you know...

CA: ...even a tiny possibility?

HC: Well you know that you're asking a very important question, and believe you me, I don't like where I am at all. This is the most grievous time of my life. I don't like to teach what I'm teaching. And if there's anything I don't want to teach, anything contrary to the Bible. And so I examine this and examine this and examine this but I can tell you that the more I study the Bible and others also—a great many people are researching this also, checking it out in the Bible. There's more and more evidence that this is where we are.

At the beginning of the call Mr. Camping indicated that he had received many letters from pastors pointing him to the truth, correcting his errant ways. But it is self-evident that Mr. Camping has placed himself beyond the realm of correction. This is the conclusion of many even within the ranks of Family Radio itself. Many who have supported the work have faced Camping and have found him entrenched. But this is not a response to the question that was asked. Saying "I don't like teaching this" is not the same as "Yes, it is possible I am in error."

> And all you have to do is look around at the churches. If you believe you still have a reasonably true church...next Sunday you go to any other church in your community. What do you think you're going to find? And this is true all through the world. And just in that way you're going to realize something terrible has happened, because it certainly wasn't this way fifty years ago. Fifty years ago there was a lot more consistent, Biblical teaching than today.

But in reality, that is just Mr. Camping's very limited viewpoint expressing itself. Surely America has seen a tremendous decline. But other nations are far better off today than they were fifty years ago, and the entire world is better of than it was in the dark days prior to the Reformation. Indeed, if there ever was a time when someone could have argued, successfully, from the evidence around them that the "church has been destroyed," it would have been around the time of the burning of Jan Hus by the Council of Constance (1415), and in the dark decades thereafter, where even Wyclif's bones were exhumed and burned in protest for his evangelical teaching! But would such an argument, based upon limited observation, fraught with ignorance of God's plans for the future, have been valid? Certainly not! God was not finished with the church then, and likewise, he is not finished with her today.

Mr. Arnzen accomplished something very valuable in his call. He asked the exact questions that needed to be asked to bring out the central elements of Camping's teaching, and his inability to provide a coherent biblical response. In God's providence Mr. Camping kept him on the line, allowing him to raise valuable topics and insightful questions. It is certain that his replies demonstrate the complete circularity of his position: one must first accept that Camping's spiritualizations have something to do with God's truth right from the start, for they are not liable to any form of biblical examination on any standards outside of Camping's own mind. He sets the rules, and once they are established, he can "answer" objections by simply dismissing them. Only the person who truly *wants* to follow Harold Camping can find that kind of argumentation convincing.

Flee Indeed:
Flee Harold Camping

There are some who have read this book with much sadness and grief in their heart. Harold Camping may well have been the one who introduced you to the gospel. You may have been very blessed by the ministry of Family Radio, its many programs, even by its high standards in music. You may have some kind of emotional or sentimental attachment to Family Radio, or even Harold Camping himself. You may feel that responding to him, and especially identifying his teachings as simply heretical, is "unkind" or "unloving."

We surely live in a day when that kind of thinking is common. It is rampant even in the church which should uphold the highest standards of truth, honesty, integrity, and dedication to God's Word. Rare is the person today who thinks with clarity and reason so as to separate the person from the issues being discussed. Instead, to identify a person's teaching as false is understood to be an attack upon the person, and everyone knows, Christians are not supposed to be "mean spirited." Today that means, "Christians are to think like the world, lack any and all backbone, and most importantly, are never, ever to place God's honor, God's truth, and God's character at the top of their list of personal priorities."

The person who loves God's truth will love God's Word. That Word reveals the body of Christ, the church, to be the object of God's special love. Christ loves the church, as husbands are to love their wives. If we follow Christ's lead and example we will love the church, serve Christ through the church, and thank God for the privilege of experiencing the fellowship of the Spirit within the community of faith. Attacks upon that body of faith will not be dismissed as mere "disagreements" anymore than an attack upon one's husband, wife, father, mother, or children, could be lightly dismissed. When one loves Christ one loves His church. And Harold Camping is proclaiming the death of that church. As such, he must be rebuked, refuted, and exposed as the false teacher he is.

A true Bible teacher consciously seeks to allow the Word to speak for itself. The *last* thing he wants to do is insert himself, his ideas, and his "insights" into the text of Scripture. Consider it well: the one given the privilege to stand in the presence of God's people and open the Word of God in the role of a teacher should realize the *sacredness* of this duty. And when we properly weigh the importance of this duty, the first desire of the heart will be to have God speak with clarity and power from the Word. Allow the Spirit to take the God-breathed words of Scripture and apply them to the hearts and minds of God's people, shining the divine light of truth throughout the believer's soul; and searching out every corner of their being, bringing repentance, encouragement, edification, and holiness. This is divine business we are privileged to engage in! The more of "self" that is put forward, the less of Christ will be heard and seen.

That same attitude of reverence and respect for the preaching of the Word will preclude anyone from adopting the attitude Harold Camping displays regarding the Scriptures. Why? Because quite simply, Harold Camping shows tremendous disrespect for the authors of Scripture and the Spirit who carried them along as they spoke from God (2 Peter 1:20–21). When a person will not attempt to determine the original meaning of a text of Scripture, we can rightly say they are being irresponsible, or even lazy. But when a person not only ignores that original meaning, but replaces it with an incoherent, arbitrary "spiritual meaning" that is nothing more than the projection of the person's own thoughts, and then has the bravado to claim that the result is actually the "real" meaning of the Word of God, such a person crosses the line not only into false teaching, but into insufferable spiritual arrogance. Does this description offend? If it does, why? If the argument is sound (and it is), can we do anything less than decry the attitude portrayed by Harold Camping in his utter and wholesale misrepresentation of the sacred Scriptures that communicate to us the very message by which we are saved?

Harold Camping is fomenting rebellion within the congregations of Christ against God's truth about the church and God's authority as it is represented, for the good of His people, in the eldership of the church. The student of church history cannot help but recall a parallel situation that developed early on in Corinth, where the rebellious members of the church rose up and cast out their elders. Was there an ancient version of Harold Camping inciting the same rebellious elements of the congregation who had given Paul so much trouble forty or fifty years earlier? We don't know, but one thing is for certain: it was important enough for the elders at Rome to write to Corinth back then. Do we love the truth less today? Is God's providential provision of the church as a place of protection, blessing, encouragement, and growth, less important today than it was in 95 A.D.? Surely not.

I would like to address four groups of possible readers in concluding this work.

■ A Word to the Faithful Believer
It is possible you have picked up this work because you love the church and love your fellow believers in the fellowship of faith, and have become concerned about what Camping has been teaching. Possibly you have experienced the loss of loved ones in your fellowship who have taken Camping's word as gospel and have "fled the church." Or perhaps you are just interested in the subject of the church, or the interpretation of the Bible, and have come to this work as a result.

In any case, it is my desire for the mature believer in Christ that there be two fundamental conclusions in your thinking as you conclude this study. First, that the means we use to interpret the text of the Scriptures is not a mere academic debate, but is in reality a vitally important area of study for *all* believers, not merely those in positions of Christian leadership. We live in an ever more hostile cultural environment, resulting in an ever increasing necessity on the part of *every* believer to engage in practical, apologetic defense of the faith. To give an answer (or to simply refute the world's contentions for the sake of your own faith) requires a knowledge of the Word of God. Accurately handling the text of Scripture requires the use of tools, and a sound hermeneutic that allows for consistent and meaningful interpretation. These are vital issues, for we use a form of hermeneutics whether we know it or not. Sadly, we normally pick up our methodology not by specific study of the subject, but by mere inference and imitation. Bad teachers tend to inculcate bad methods of interpretation in their followers even if they never mention such words as "exegesis" or "hermeneutics." Likewise, sound teachers communicate good methods of interpretation, though they are much more likely to see the importance of formally introducing the subject and teaching upon it openly.

Second, the church needs *churchmen*. We need faithful believers who will stand in the gap, unashamedly reject the popular view of the day (look for a church that is "comfy" and "undemanding" that provides "programs" and a latte bar in the foyer, but that does not call for commitment, dedication, sacrifice, and never, ever preaches the unpopular truths of the gospel like God's wrath against sin, or the necessity of self-denial for the disciple of Christ), and commit themselves to loving the brethren within the context of service to Christ, all to the glory of God. The church is despised in our world, but far too often, for all the wrong reasons. The church that seeks friendship with the world through compromise only brings disrespect upon itself. The world knows compromise when it sees it. When a church defines itself, its message, its worship, not on what is pleasing to God, but what is pleasing to the natural man, it has obviously developed serious flaws in its theology and teaching. Such churches do not inspire in the disciple of Christ a desire for sacrificial service to Christ within its walls. But the fellowship that refuses to adopt the ways of the world, refuses to compromise its message so as to be "politically correct," seeks to order itself in the light of God's Word; and places as its first and foremost priority the proclamation of the entirety of God's truth, calling for the deepest devotion of the regenerate heart. What's more, these congregations of Christ must hear the call of the Spirit in our day.

■ To Those Who Believe Harold Camping

You must realize that you have, in essence, replaced biblical authority with the authority of Harold Camping. That is why I have often used the phrase *Solus Campingus* when pointing out the constant fact that Camping's entire argument turns upon unfounded assertions that "this means this" or "that represents that." Without the ultimate authority of Harold Camping as the vessel through which the "true spiritual meaning" of the text is somehow brought to the rest of us, his entire system collapses. Of course he does not openly claim to be a prophet or inspired: but if your entire system puts your followers in the position of treating you as if you are, why bother with the open proclamation? If you already have so much authority over others that they will leave their churches at your command and sit around a radio so as to be taught by you, how much more power do you really need?

It is highly doubtful that any of you began your journey with the specific intent in mind, "I'd like to replace sound biblical authority in my life with something way off base. Now how do I do that?" You probably found in Harold Camping a voice that was willing to say some unpopular things. At first there were things he said that did not make sense, but over time, you became accustomed to him and to his views, even adopting them as your own. Maybe you lived through the 1994 debacle and backed away, only to be drawn back over time. Maybe you only came to start listening to Camping since 1994. It is possible you struggled greatly when Camping began to introduce this new teaching, but as you continued to listen, continued to hear argument after argument, you finally began to wonder if maybe he wasn't right. Maybe those things that bother you about your church are indicative of the end of the church age after all?

Falling under the spell of false teaching rarely happens over night. Some people, to be sure, are unstable in all their ways, are blown about by every wind of doctrine, and hence latch onto every strange permutation of theology that is offered by man. But many of those who have embraced Camping's new doctrine did so to the surprise of all of those around them. It took him time to convince them of his view. Maybe you fall into this group. If so, please consider the following statements.

Harold Camping cannot demonstrate that his teachings actually carry the authority of the Bible, for as soon as he says, "this is a picture of this," he has left the inspired text behind and is now simply giving you the imaginations of his own heart. Why should you believe that he, and he alone, in this case, has "the" insight? Has God's Spirit worked so poorly that he cannot lead other Christian leaders, men who know far more about Scripture than Camping does, to the same conclusions?

Harold Camping cannot provide you with spiritual guidance and protection. By calling you to flee from the churches he is, in fact, placing your soul in great danger. And for what reason? The only reason that can be seen is that he desires to have people follow him as a religious leader. Is that sufficient reason?

Finally, realize that someday Harold Camping is going to be gone, and his teaching will pass away. The "fellowships" will end. The day will come when you will realize that you must face the fact that just as many bought into Camping's 1994 debacle, so too this new teaching was a flash-in-the-pan teaching that had no basis, no future, no divine authority. Indeed, there may be some who bought into *both* teachings. In any case, your duty is clear. No matter what the level of embarrassment you will experience, the truth of the Word of God has not changed, and will not change even with the passing of Harold Camping. You must have the fortitude to repent of your deception, embrace the biblical truth, and place yourself back under the leadership that you have, temporarily, rejected. Will those men need to speak to you about your discernment? Yes, they will; and God will use that correction to your betterment.

In any case, I plead with you: hear the Word of the Lord, recognize the truth it proclaims with such clarity about the church, and for the sake of truth, turn off that radio and quit following the counsel of a mere man!

■ To The Not Yet Convinced Listener

If you listen to Harold Camping regularly, but are not yet convinced of his teachings on this subject, please consider: When the Bible specifically and directly addresses the church, you *never* find anything that remotely resembles the fanciful conclusions of Harold Camping. You hear much about the perpetuity of the church, God's purposes in the church, but you don't find the apostles relying on turning Sennacharib into Satan or identifying every possible beast in apocalyptic literature as the devil, or making everything from apocalyptic witnesses to Hebrew kings into pictures of the church, etc. They spoke plainly and clearly, and any person who overturns their plain teaching of the Bible for the allegorical spiritualizations of Harold Camping is bound to err. Stay the course, examine his teachings for consistency; and when you don't find it, look elsewhere for your spiritual edification than Harold Camping.

■ A Final Word to the Elders of the Church

Those who minister faithfully in the church cannot help but find this newest challenge to the peace of the church a tremendously frustrating thing. This is especially true of the pastor who has faithfully sought to model sound biblical interpretation and spiritual maturity, only to find long-time members of the flock falling for Camping's erroneous teachings. It is enough to make one consider finding another line of work.

There are two important issues I wish to leave with the elders of the church. First, do not be discouraged by this trial. There will be more to come. A wise minister friend once said to me when I was but a young person entering into the field, "If you ever get your eyes off the Shepherd and onto the sheep, you will burn out of the ministry in no time." You can teach, pray, labor and work, and if you measure your effort solely on what you can observe in the lives of particular individuals, it can be quite discouraging. When we live in a culture that does not respect truth and that is under the judgment of God, we must first and foremost focus upon honoring and pleasing Him. He has told us what our duty is, and when we do that work with a cheerful heart, He sees, He knows, and He is glorified.

Secondly, if you have lost people to this movement, start thinking even now how you will handle their eventual reappearance. This movement cannot long last. It has no foundation, and as any building so poorly constructed, it will collapse under its own weight. These people will return. You have to make sure they know they can come to you in repentance. You need to walk a very difficult line, for you must see fruits of repentance (what they are doing is, in fact, sinful, even though they may well be deceived themselves), you must speak to their lack of discernment, but at the same time, you must make sure they know they will not encounter your pride when they return, but only a shepherd thankful to see God working in their lives. This is not an easy balance to maintain, but we must seek to both announce it, and live it consistently.

■

■ Notes

Before the Battle Begins

1. There is much discussion concerning the identity of the "rulers and authorities in heavenly places." Most view these as spiritual forces opposed to God and His work in the world, hence, the church demonstrates to God's spiritual enemies His wisdom in joining Jew and Gentile together in their common salvation in Christ.

2. These would be the translations based upon the *Textus Receptus*, which has a minor textual variant wherein it differs from the more commonly used Nestle-Aland text platform.

The Importance and Role of Church Membership

1. Ironically, Roman Catholic apologists repeatedly assert that the diversity in Protestant beliefs is actually due to *sola scriptura*, a belief they decry and deny. But in reality, it is just the opposite: those groups that purposefully and knowingly seek to be obedient to the rule of Scripture, eschew outside authorities, and listen obediently to *all* that the Scriptures teach are far more united on the central issues of the faith than any and all groups that do not.

2. This is surely not the first time in history when truth has languished in the minority. Many centuries have passed when God's judgment upon nations or empires has manifested itself in withdrawing from the people a growing, vital witness to Christ in the church. A healthy and growing church is a blessing upon any nation, a blessing of grace. No nation ever deserves such a blessing. But it is short-sightedness that allows anyone to look at a particular situation in a particular time, see God's judgment coming upon a people, and extrapolate from this the idea that the church has come to an end or is destroyed.

The Church Age Has Ended?

1. One of the most dangerous elements of Camping's teaching is his mixture of truth and error. We would strongly agree with him that the violation of the clear teaching of Scripture regarding the nature of the eldership (positively expressed in 1 Timothy 3:1–7 and Titus 1:6-11 and negatively in 1 Cor. 14:34–35 and 1 Timothy 2:11-14) amounts to a violation of God's right to rule over His own church.

2. Here Camping is drawing from his Reformed heritage and presenting as a "high place" the Arminian doctrine of universal atonement, specifically, that the Lord Jesus died substituationarily in the place of each and every person with the intention of saving each and every person. Camping's position is that of Reformed theology, specifically, that Christ died substituationarily in the place of His elect people, not each and every

141

person. We have defended this view in other publications (such as *The Potter's Freedom*, pp. 229–282). We are very quick to emphasize that while we would generally agree with Camping's views on the extent and purpose of the atonement, we come to that belief by the solid, consistent exegesis of the Scriptures. Camping did not come to the conclusions he has on the atonement by using the same kind of allegorical interpretation upon which he bases his unorthodox views.

3. I.e., the idea that baptism brings about regeneration. Reformed believers would agree that this is an error, over against some Protestant denominations that continue to hold to this error.

4. This is a strange view of Harold Camping whereby he denies that faith is used as a means by God in His decree of salvation of His elect. This is an error on his part where he mistakenly thinks that if God uses faith as a means that this somehow results in the addition of a human work to salvation. The ability to exercise saving faith is a gift given by God to His elect people in the work of regeneration.

5. This would seemingly be in reference to premillenialism. Given how very strange and inconsistent Camping's own eschatology is, this truly seems like an example of the pot calling the kettle black.

6. Another strange Campingism in light of the plain teaching of Jesus in Matthew 19:9 and the fact that in God's law virtual divorces were given on the basis of every single capital crime (i.e., a person would be "divorced" from their spouse if that spouse was executed for the commission of any of the capital crimes under the law).

7. Harold Camping, *Has the Era of the Church Age Come to an End?* (Family Stations, Inc., Oakland, CA) n.d., p. 12.

8. He often speaks of "other ministries like Family Radio," but he never mentions any by name, and surely, we know of none that believe as Harold Camping believes regarding his list of "high places," hence one is left wondering if in fact the only ones left preaching the "true" gospel are those operating under the name "Family Radio."

9. Note again the uselessness of this kind of allegorical interpretation. These two witnesses are said in the earlier verses to have the ability to consume anyone who wants to hurt them with fire. When has the church had such a capacity? And Camping does not go on to the fact that these two witnesses are raised back to life after three and a half days. Is the church going to be re-established on the earth in light of this? It does not do him any good to point to the distinction between the eternal/invisible church and the temporal/visible church, as if the two witnesses, since they are taken up to heaven, represent solely the invisible church after their resurrection. The resurrection takes place *on earth* prior to their resurrection to heaven. Harold Camping simply does not bother himself with details such as these.

Hearing God Accurately

1. Of course, non-written forms of "revelation" are much less able to stand the test of time. Those systems that claim an oral tradition alone cannot establish the historical nature of the tradition. Such a non-written tradition is subject to radical change over time, while written tradition leaves a documentary record that can either demonstrate change or prove that the content has not, in fact, changed over time (this is the case with the Christian Scriptures, whose historical pedigree and documentation is unparalleled). Oral tradition is likewise liable to a wide variety of interpretations that are precluded in written sources due to the rules of grammar, syntax, and the study of the historical meaning of words, etc.

2. "End of the Church Age #2" at www.familyradio.com, beginning at 37:53.

3. See Walter Kaiser and Moises Silva, *An Introduction to Biblical Hermeneutics* (Zondervan, 1994) as an excellent introductory text.

4. The theories that posit Hebrew or Aramaic originals of various of the New Testament books are unconvincing and lacking historical support.

5. The necessity and centrality of original language study for ministers and those in positions of teaching and writing has been a given in the vast majority of Christian denominations since the Reformation. Only in recent decades in the United States has the emphasis upon these studies declined, or in some cases, been denied.

6. We must differentiate between the nature of Scripture as an inspired revelation and the work of the Holy Spirit in enlightening the mind of the obedient believer who wishes to understand, love, and apply the Scriptures. The Holy Spirit applies the unchanging and eternal truths of Scripture within the context of our lives, but this does not involve the creation of a "spiritual" or "allegorical" meaning of the text.

Harold Camping Examined

1. Actually, many of the "asheriim" were merely places of idolatrous worship in a grove of trees with no elaborate structure associated with it. This is yet another example of a Campingism; a willingness to emphasize a point at the sacrifice of the truth itself, all to promote his own personal ideas and theology.

2. Since Camping goes on to mention consistories and synods, we will assume he meant to say "New Testament era," not the New Testament proper.

3. This quotation comes from the Open Forum discussion detailed in the chapter "The Debate That Almost Was."

Dangerous Airwaves: Harold Camping Teaches on Family Radio

1. The specific URL to the recording of this quoted material, as of the time of this writing, is http://216.231.22.150:7080/ramgen/family/class/class_25.rm. The title given to the file is 2001 Missions Springs Conference, Harold Camping, Part II. The entire thirteen part series by Camping can be found, currently, at: http://www.familyradio.com/original/realaudio/class.htm. We begin our quotations around the 37:53 mark and conclude at the 47:50 mark.

The Debate That Almost Was

1. And that includes John 21, as we have seen.

2. Indeed, without elders to provide discernment and guidance, one could say Mr. Camping's "fellowship" concept is far more liable to all the criticisms he makes of the church in comments such as this.

3. Camping denies the instrumental role of faith, seemingly thinking this would lead to rank synergism, the joining of the actions of God with the actions of man. He is surely aware of the Reformed response to this: that the act of faith is not the action of an autonomous will, but a divine gift, an enablement that accompanies the work of regeneration itself. Such is to simply recognize that God ordains the ends as well as the means. Faith in Christ, which is everywhere noted as the sole means of obtaining eternal life, is part of God's ordained means of bringing His elect to the fullness of their relationship with Christ.

4. We have already noted, and responded to, the assertion that the Holy Spirit is not active in the church in our previous presentation.

5. 2 Peter 3:16